Classroom *Connections*

Strategies for Integrated Learning

KATH MURDOCH

ELEANOR CURTAIN
PUBLISHING

Link ESPL
831-14

First published in 1998

Eleanor Curtain Publishing
906 Malvern Road
Armadale Vic 3134
Australia

National Library of Australia CIP

Murdoch, Kath.
   Classroom connections: strategies for integrated learning

   Bibliography.
   Includes index.
   ISBN 1 875327 48 7.

   1. Interdisciplinary approach in education – Australia. 2. Primary school teaching – Australia. 3. Education, Primary – Australia. 4. Lesson planning – Australia. I. Title.

327.1020994

Production by Publishing Solutions Pty Ltd
Edited by Ruth Siems
Cover design by David Constable
Cover photograph by Sara Curtain
Printed in Australia
by Shannon Books

Dedication

This book is dedicated, in loving memory, to my son
Callum Ian Murdoch Ray
whose short life taught me so much

and to all the children and their teachers – from whom I continue to learn.

ACKNOWLEDGMENTS

I am always heartened by the enthusiastic and generous way that teachers, when given the opportunity, share their practice with each other. I hope this book contributes in some way to this process of sharing – of recycling and refining 'best practice' in classrooms – and that it encourages teachers to reflect on, add to and improve their repertoire within the context of an integrated approach.

I would like to thank several people for their assistance in the development of this book. The ideas within it have been trialled and discussed with teachers and children in numerous schools around Australia. I wish to acknowledge the contributions those children and teachers have made to the development of my own repertoire of teaching strategies for integrated learning. Some samples of their work appear throughout the book.

My gratitude, in particular, to the staff from four schools who trialled activities and responded to the manuscript:

Glen Katherine Primary School
Ringwood Heights Primary School
St Anthony's Primary School
Sunshine North Primary School

For several years, I have been fortunate to work with some outstanding teachers and students in the Faculty of Education at Melbourne University. I acknowledge the role these colleagues have played in helping shape my understandings and my teaching skills. I also continue to learn much from the wisdom and experience of my school-based colleagues Debbie Sukarna, Lesley Wing Jan, Jo ann Parry and fellow consultant David Hornsby.

Finally, a special thankyou to my husband, Stephen Ray, for his patient support throughout the project.

CONTENTS

INTRODUCTION

The case for integrated curriculum

Much has been written in recent times about the benefits of an integrated curriculum – for both teachers and learners. These writers argue that skills, values and understandings are best taught and assessed within meaningful, 'connected' contexts. (See, for example, Beane 1991, Harste 1992, Pigdon & Woolley 1992, Hamston and Murdoch 1996, Wilson 1991, Fogarty 1993, Perkins 1993, Hayes-Jacobs 1989, and Murdoch & Hornsby 1997.) Integrated units of work, based around topics of relevance and interest to students, are one vehicle for providing such planned contexts for learning.

While various planning models for and approaches to integrated curriculum have been put forward, there is general agreement about the value of helping learners make connections within and across key learning areas. Integrated curriculum is said to advantage teachers and learners by:

- **reflecting**, more closely, the interdependence between all aspects of life in the real world

- **challenging** learners to use and develop their thinking skills as they work to make connections and see 'the big picture'

- **catering** to the various learning styles and preferences held by students

- **managing** an increasingly crowded curriculum

- **meeting** outcomes in context

- **making** more 'sense' to the school day – as activities have stronger links with each other

- **providing** students with a greater degree of control over their learning

- **encouraging** staff to plan and work in teams

- **structuring** a meaningful context for the teaching and assessment of outcomes across key learning areas

- **enabling** students to transfer knowledge, skills and values across content and experiences

- **skilling** students to process and respond to experiences in a range of ways

- **linking** purposes with activities more explicitly

- **enriching** understanding, enjoyment and reflection in teaching and learning

WORKING WITHIN THE BIG PICTURE

For several years, a group of teaching staff based at the University of Melbourne's Faculty of Education have worked with a model for integrated curriculum that promotes a 'big picture' approach to planning. Over time, this model has been explored, discussed, modified and shaped by many classroom teachers committed to developing students' understanding of the 'way the world works'.

The theoretical underpinnings of this model have been explored in detail elsewhere (Pigdon & Woolley 1992, Hamston & Murdoch 1996, and Murdoch & Hornsby 1997). This book is designed to complement such publications by providing a collection of practical strategies to support teachers' planning and teaching of integrated units of work. Readers unfamiliar with the model are encouraged to refer to the work of the above writers; however, a brief overview is provided here.

The essence of this approach to planning is the relationship between those learning areas concerned with 'the world around us' (science, technology, health, and environmental and social education) and those areas *through* which we explore and come to understand that world (language, mathematics, art, drama, dance, music and aspects of technology). Units of work are planned around topics of substance (drawn from science, SOSE, technology and health) and, as students investigate these topics, they develop increasingly sophisticated understandings of their world.

A MODEL FOR INTEGRATED CURRICULUM

The figure opposite describes a model for integrated curriculum. In this model, the starting point for planning is the content associated with the learning areas of science, social and environmental education, health and technology. Together, these areas deal with 'life experience'. They contain the **rich concepts** that drive effective learning. While real-life experience is not neatly categorised into 'social/biological/physical ...', organising curriculum in this way is a helpful means of achieving balance; we know what it is we are integrating.

The curriculum areas in the right-hand box are those through which children come to make sense of their world. Language, for example, is the vehicle through which so much of our daily experience is processed. We depend on our ability to use language, mathematics and the arts in order to inquire, gather information, analyse and communicate our understandings to others. In this way, there is no 'competition' between learning areas. One area cannot be seen as more important than another because each is integral to the other. The 'subjects' that deal with the social, physical, biological and personal worlds give substance and meaning to the forms of perception and expression. In turn, the forms of expression and perception enable us to make sense of life experience.

Each form of expression and perception has distinctive processes and conventions. Children must develop mastery of these in order to be efficient learners. If we don't help children to learn the processes and conventions, we don't help them to express themselves. These conventions are best taught in

Developing understandings about the world – physical, social, biological, etc (the 'content' areas)

Processes and their conventions

Forms of expression and perception

Language – English
– **LOTE** (languages other than English)

Listening, speaking, reading, viewing and writing … *and their conventions*

Mathematics

Estimating, measuring, subtracting … *and their conventions*

The Arts (visual and performing)

Viewing, painting, sculpting, dancing, composing, acting … *and their conventions*

Technology (some aspects)

Investigating, designing, producing, evaluation … *and their conventions*

PE (movement)

Dancing, moving, performing, gymnastics … *and their conventions*

Cooperating and interacting

Reasoning and reflecting

Imagining and inquiring

Assessing and evaluating

Studies of society & the environment

Science

Some aspects of **Technology**

Health and some aspects of **PE**

and the ways of thinking and working relevant to each area

A climate and classroom environment that supports learning

A model for integrated curriculum (from an original concept by Pigdon & Woolley)

the broader context of an integrated program because their purposes become much clearer to the learner. In this model, the integrated program helps the teacher to determine the most appropriate context for teaching many of the conventions and processes, although there will be times when these conventions are, necessarily, taught outside the integrated framework.

The four threads that underpin this model indicate the 'ways of working' that facilitate the learning process for students and, ultimately, help to ensure that connections are made. The model, then, becomes not only an explanation of the relationship between 'subjects' but an approach to teaching and learning characterised by inquiry, reflection, cooperation and ongoing assessment and evaluation.

TOWARDS UNDERSTANDING

Based on their understanding of students' needs, interests, prior knowledge and experiences, teachers plan a set of broad understandings to help frame a unit of work. These understandings – though specific to the topic – incorporate some of the key concepts that students explore with increasing sophistication as they move through school. The set of understandings below were written for a group of 8- and 9-year-olds. The integrated unit of work focused on the issue of caring for waterways. Some of the broad concepts are highlighted:

- **Living things**, including humans, **depend** on water for their survival.
- For some living things, **water environments** provide important food and **habitat**.
- As it moves through its **cycle**, water is **changed** by both natural events and human activities. Many of these human activities cause **pollution**.
- There are **systems** that have been set up to carry waste and excess water. **Pollutants** that enter these systems eventually end up in the sea.
- Because it is essential to life, water needs to be **conserved** and protected from pollution.
- There are ways we can **modify** our lifestyle to help protect and conserve water – for humans and for the other animals and plants which depend on it.

INQUIRY AS A FRAMEWORK FOR PLANNING

Inquiry as a framework for developing understandings about the world has a long history in educational pedagogy and remains a powerful tool in the contemporary classroon. Recently produced 'outcomes-based' curriculum documents (for example, the Victorian *Curriculum Standards Framework* in Australia (1995), or the Florida *Curriculum Framework* (1996) in the USA) continue to advocate the process of inquiry as a vehicle for achieving effective learning in areas such as science, health, and social and environmental education. The inquiry approach reflects the belief that *active* involvement on the part of students in constructing their knowledge is essential to effective teaching and learning. Inquiry methodology and integrated curriculum are also supported by recent research into 'brain-based learning'. Caine and Caine (1990) argue, for instance, that as the brain seeks pattern, meaning and connectedness, methods that move from rote memorisation to meaning-centred learning are ultimately much more successful. They note that the brain has a 'natural capacity for integration' and that this should be invoked by the teaching methods used in the classroom.

It is argued that curriculum needs to be a 'collaborative process in which teachers and students have a voice' (Short et al. 1996). The emphasis in the inquiry approach moves from the view that knowledge is something that is 'taught' to knowledge as *learned*. The inquiry approach encourages students, through active investigation, to unify, rather than separate knowledge as they move from the acquisition of facts to the development of broader concepts and generalisations. It opens up channels of investigation which subject-specific curriculum may otherwise close and emphasises the learning of fundamental principles and concepts – the 'big ideas' (Hamston & Murdoch 1996).

In the classroom, inquiry learning parallels other student-centred and process-oriented curriculum developments such as whole language (Goodman 1996, Harste, Woodward & Burke 1984, Cambourne 1988), negotiated curriculum (Boomer 1992) and philosophy for children (Lipman 1988, Splitter 1995). In short, the focus in inquiry is centred on *process* as well as content.

In this model for planning integrated units, a ***sequence*** of activities and experiences is developed to build on and challenge student perceptions. This sequence is inquiry-based in that it begins with students' prior knowledge and experience and moves through a deliberate process wherein that knowledge is extended, challenged, and refined. During this process, students and teachers draw on a range of resources and work across key learning areas. The sequence of activities has been grouped under the following broad headings:

- tuning in
- finding out
- sorting out
- going further
- making connections
- taking action

This sequence of planning phases, and the strategies suggested for each one, are based on the belief that learning is more effective when the points highlighted below are acknowledged and acted on.

- **Prior knowledge and experience** are recognised, made explicit and actively built upon.

- Students see a **real purpose** for what they are learning.

- Students come to understand more about their **own process of learning**

- Students are as **directly involved** as possible in gathering information first hand.

- Students are given opportunities to process experiences in a **range of ways**.

- Teachers recognise that students will **construct their knowledge in different ways**.

- Students have some **choice and opportunities to follow paths of interest** and need.

- The links between **theory and action** are made clear.

- The **purposes** for activities are made explicit.

- Planned activities and experiences recognise the interaction between **knowledge, skills, beliefs, values and personal expectations**.

- **Risk-taking** is encouraged.

- Learning is pursued without the unnecessary **restriction of subject boundaries**.

- Students are given time to **reflect** on their learning.

- Students learn in an environment where their **self-esteem** is nutured.

(Atkin 1997; Munro 1993; Osborne & Freyberg 1986; Baird & Mitchell 1986)

The strategies in this book are, therefore, learner centred rather than subject centred and have a wide range of applications.

It's not just what you plan – it's the way that you teach it!

While more attention has been given in recent times to planning models for integrated curriculum, teachers require ongoing support in the transfer between planning and *practice*. The success of integrated curriculum ultimately depends on the nature of its actual *implementation* in the classroom. As well as attending to the connections between the learning areas involved, teaching strategies employed in any unit should, in themselves, help students to make links. That is what this book is all about – it is designed to help teachers and learners build up a *repertoire of 'integrative' strategies*. This repertoire can then be drawn on and continually refined as units are planned and carried out. This integrated approach to curriculum can, therefore, be seen as having three key elements:

When planning an integrated unit, the teacher:

⬇

- selects a significant topic and develops understandings (from SOSE, Science, Health and Technology) to drive the unit

⬇

- uses an inquiry framework to select and sequence learning experiences across key learning areas

⬇

- employs a range of strategies to help learners make connections and develop understandings, skills and values

THE USE OF THE TERM 'STRATEGY'

The term 'strategy' has been adopted to describe the various teaching procedures and activities outlined in this book. The use of the term is deliberate because it can also refer to the learning experience of students. For example, concept mapping as a teaching strategy becomes, with practice, a learning strategy that students can use in a range of situations. The term 'strategy' also suggests something purposeful, a means to an end, a thoughtful, planned process designed to achieve a desired, meaningful outcome.

WHY DEVELOP A REPERTOIRE OF STRATEGIES?

> Teachers for the 21st century will need the tools to make conscious decisions about their teaching … [they] must be able to read qualitative information in action and think on their feet to provide instruction that respects the preferences and learning styles of individuals …
>
> (Behar-Horenstein 1994, p.46)

Despite advances in research on effective teaching and learning, many teachers feel less confident about the practical application of strategies in the classroom context. In short – what we know is not always reflected in what we do. For some, the strategies suggested in this book will require a reconceptualisation of what it means to teach and to learn. Where past practice has favored more passive approaches, our knowledge about learning demands that we employ a more diverse, active range of strategies in our repertoire. (Goodlad 1983, Gardner 1983, Feden 1994)

The benefits of using a wide range of strategies in teaching are many. Perhaps the most powerful reason is the extent to which this can better meet the diversity of student needs and learning styles. Different strategies demand different ways of working – some strategies will access or promote a particular student's understanding better than others. If one of the goals of integrated curriculum is to assist students to develop a 'big picture' understanding of their world – then we must **teach in a way that promotes understanding** (not just the recall of facts). The strategies in this book – together with the overall framework for unit planning – are designed to promote understanding. It is argued that effective learning comes about when teachers engage students in strategies that employ different 'processing modes'. The deliberate use of strategies that stimulate a range of 'ways of knowing' helps students to make meaning. (Atkin 1993; 1997)

Developing a varied repertoire also means that, as teachers, we enhance our capacity to transfer teaching skills to different contexts, be they created by changes in age levels, topics, classrooms or resources. We need to be aware of the decisions we make as we teach – to draw on the approaches, resources and techniques that will work best in a given context. This flexibility in teaching mirrors the kind of flexibility we hope to engender in our students. Increasingly, society demands people who can transfer and adapt – who are able to apply something they have learned in one context to another. Creativity and problem-solving skills are necessary tools for navigating our way through life. The strategies in this book are designed to add to both teachers' and students' 'tool kit' for investigating and understanding this complex world.

Using this book

MAKING A MEAL OUT OF PLANNING

This book provides you with a guide to strategies that can be employed at various stages of a unit of work. Use it rather like a menu – if the unit of work is a 'meal', then each section can be seen as a course, with a selection of ideas from which to choose. Each section deals with one phase of unit planning (although there are some strategies that can be used across the phases or stages of a unit and these are noted in the text). While the phases themselves are less linear and separate in reality, it is important to keep this broad sequence in mind when planning. The strategies suggested are designed to enhance the particular kinds of learning purposes that underpin each phase.

The strategies are generic in nature, easily modified for different age levels and topics, and examples of this are provided throughout. Variations on the basic procedure are provided for most strategies, which will help teachers to transfer the strategy to their particular topic, age group and setting. In addition to the ideas for each phase of inquiry, there are several strategies for sharing, discussing and reflecting on learning which can be used throughout each unit. Sample units are also provided to demonstrate the way in which strategies from each stage work together to enhance planning.

You are encouraged to add to the menu. The blank strategy proformas can be filled in as you discover new ways of working in an integrated curriculum. Staff meetings might include opportunities for you to share your own strategy ideas. Display your menu in the staff room or wherever you meet to plan your units.

HOW THE STRATEGIES ARE PRESENTED

No attempt has been made to include all strategies. That would be impossible! The strategies selected have been trialled by practising teachers in many different classrooms. They are strategies that work. Some will be old favorites; others will be new. They have originated from a wide variety of sources. Some of these are published, and every effort has been made to acknowledge their source. Others have been developed and adapted over years of working with teachers and children in integrated curriculum.

Chapters 1–6 correspond to a stage of unit development. The broad purposes of each stage are identified, with more specific purposes for each strategy noted where appropriate. Chapter 7 includes strategies for sharing and reflecting on learning. These strategies are applicable throughout a unit of work. For each strategy, a basic procedure, alternatives and teaching points are provided. Many also include examples and possible applications.

Chapter 9 provides a summary of all strategies, presented in checklist form. This can be used for record-keeping purposes and will also help you to locate the strategies.

CHOOSING THE RIGHT STRATEGY

There are no simple rules for the selection of strategies. Your knowledge of the needs and skills of your students, together with the aims of your unit, will be your best guide. Generally, the choice of strategies will depend on the following factors:

- the broad understandings underpinning the unit
- the particular stage of the unit you have reached and your key purposes at that time
- the skills that you and your students already have and those you wish to develop
- the strategies students have used in the past (in each unit, you should revise some and introduce others)
- the age levels, abilities and learning preferences of the students with whom you are working
- the nature of the information and resources with which students are working
- the resources and facilities available to you
- your own teaching style and the learning styles of the students with whom you are working

An environment that supports learning

The strategies suggested in this book are based on several assumptions about the process of teaching and learning. Such beliefs underpin a classroom environment in which students feel valued. The relationship between the teacher and students and among students themselves must be a positive and respectful one if these strategies are to achieve their full potential. The use of the strategies themselves will go some way towards achieving this climate, but other aspects of the classroom program and environment need to be considered. A classroom environment that supports learning is characterised by:

- organisational structures (eg timetabling) that allows sufficient time for students to process and practise what they have learned

- explicit teaching styles – where teachers share their 'agenda' with students and where students are conscious of why they are doing what they are doing

- shared responsibilities – everyone contributes to the day-to-day maintenance of the physical and social environment

- mutual respect between students and teacher

- clear expectations, rules and procedures for behavior management that have been negotiated with students

- an openness to and involvement with parents and other members of the school community

- valuing each student's interests, expertise and background

- a physical set-up that allows for as much independent student activity and movement as possible: for example, easy access to materials; tables organised in groups as well as areas available for independent work; independent procedures for book borrowing; seeing the teacher; storage of books, bags and personal items; and procedures for various routines displayed around the room

- regular and constructive feedback given from teacher to student, between students and from students to teacher

- regular opportunities for students to work collaboratively as well as opportunities for them to work on their own

STRATEGIES

for tuning in

BROAD PURPOSES

- to find out what students already know, think and feel about the topic
- to provide students with a focus for the forthcoming experiences
- to provide students with opportunities to become engaged with the topic
- to ascertain the students' questions about and interest in the topic
- to allow students to share their personal experience of the topic
- to help plan further experiences and activities

About this stage of a unit

What do I already know about this aspect of the world? How do I feel about it? How have I come to know and feel these things? What am I interested in finding out about? How can I find out? What do my friends know and think about this? How is this relevant to me? These are the sorts of questions that guide student learning in the first phase of an inquiry-based unit investigation.

The activities planned for the first phase of a unit can 'make or break' the investigation to follow. The way in which the unit begins has a major impact on students' interest and involvement. Importantly, the first phase of a unit provides you with valuable data for assessment and evaluation. The strategies suggested in this chapter enable you to 'tap into' the learners' prior knowledge, interests, experiences, misconceptions and understandings. Importantly, this is a stage where students' 'misconceptions' are often revealed. Recent research, particularly in the areas of science and mathematics, has demonstrated the rather 'stubborn' nature of students' misconceptions and the degree to which they are often unmoved despite an abundance of activities and experience that might contradict their view. Part of the process of challenging and addressing these misconceptions is to make them explicit – so that the students themselves have, in a sense, 'laid their cards on the table' at the beginning of the unit. Whether misconceptions are revealed through writing, drawing, models, mind maps or discussion – a record of them is important so that they can be continually challenged and refined as the unit progresses. (White & Gunstone 1992, Osborne & Freyberg 1985, Novak & Gowin 1984)

Many of the products of strategies at the tuning in stage become an important reference point for assessment as the unit unfolds, it also helps you fine tune the direction of the unit, select appropriate resources and modify your plans.

The learning students bring to an investigation determines much of what they take from it. The tuning-in phase of a unit is very learner focused. During these activities, the teacher's role is, primarily, to stimulate, question, record, mediate and, above all, to listen. These activities are largely about sharing information, feelings, ideas and questions students already have rather than introducing them to new experiences. Shorte and Harste (1996) remind us that the inquiry cycle must begin with the student's own life experience and build from there. It is these personal experiences that lay the foundation for the broader exploration to follow.

The activities presented here aim to gauge prior knowledge and interest using a range of techniques. These techniques are deliberately varied to ensure that preferred learning styles are catered for and that you give students maximum opportunities to show what they already know and feel. The student who is not confident using oral language may, for example, reveal more about their prior knowledge through visual art or movement. In any unit of work, it is suggested that students carry out several of these activities before moving on to finding out.

One of the most important elements of the tuning-in phase is the generation of questions for investigation. While some of the strategies included in this chapter focus specifically on the development of questions, you will find that others create a climate from which questions naturally arise. Many students will begin a topic without a clear idea of what it is they want to know more about. As they are 'tuned in' to the topic, questions begin to emerge, and such questions should be recorded, revisited and refined throughout the unit of work.

> If I had to reduce all of educational philosophy to just one principle, I would say this: the most important single factor influencing learning is what the learner already knows. (Ausubel 1968, p. iv)

Brainstorming

Generally, brainstorming allows students to freely generate many ideas about a topic or problem. The essence of effective brainstorming is providing an atmosphere where all ideas are accepted and where students feel confident to express themselves. Brainstorming can often form the basis for more structured activities to follow, such as mind maps, bundling, statements, questions and topic wheels.

BASIC PROCEDURE

Brainstorming is now a popular strategy to use when beginning a unit of work, but it is not always carried out effectively. One common problem is that certain students may dominate the discussion while others rarely contribute. A whole-class brainstorm is rarely, in fact, whole class. It often represents the ideas of a small group of vocal or confident students. Following are several variations on the brainstorming strategy.

- Announce the topic, word, phrase or problem to be brainstormed, for example:

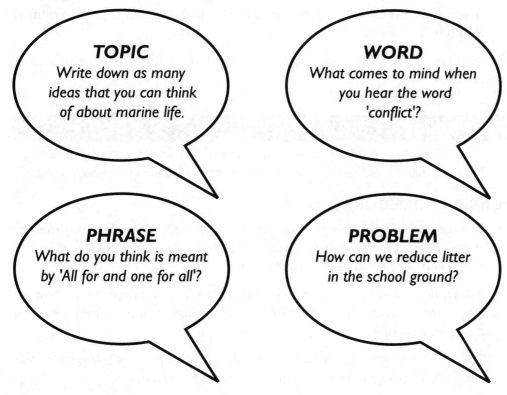

TOPIC
Write down as many ideas that you can think of about marine life.

WORD
What comes to mind when you hear the word 'conflict'?

PHRASE
What do you think is meant by 'All for and one for all'?

PROBLEM
How can we reduce litter in the school ground?

MODIFICATIONS

- Each student spends a few minutes jotting their own ideas down and then brings them to the whole group. Instead of 'hands up' for suggestions, the teacher asks specific students to read out a word from their list.

- Before the whole class is asked to contribute, ask students to talk to the person next to them about their ideas. This will help prepare them to contribute to the whole class.

- Provide individuals, pairs or small groups with strips of card. Words are brainstormed onto the cards and then pinned on the board.

- Seat students in a circle. Each child then offers one word to the list. If they cannot think of one, they may say 'pass' to allow them more time to think before being asked again in a few minutes.

- Students can brainstorm in teams before sharing with the whole class.

- Provide each team with a different aspect of the topic to brainstorm.

- Select a poem, passage from a book, picture, or piece of music relevant to the topic and have students brainstorm their response.

TEACHING POINTS

- Provide a time limit for the brainstorm.

- State a clear rule that all ideas are to be accepted without criticism.

- Once the brainstorm is complete, students can then work to prioritise or classify the ideas.

- Keep a record of ideas generated. This may be added to and modified throughout the unit.

- Students should be encouraged to record their ideas in words and/or pictures.

Bundling

This popular strategy is an excellent way to assess the related vocabulary students bring to a topic. It can form the basis for concept development throughout a unit.

BASIC PROCEDURE

- Provide individuals or groups of students with a set of small cards or paper strips. (It is a good idea to have a supply of these ready to use in the classroom. Reuse one-sided paper.)

- Ask students to brainstorm words about the topic and then write them on the strips. Words can come from whole-class brainstorming or from individual groups.

- The cards are then 'bundled' to classify ideas that belong together. Ask students to group words that seem to 'belong together'.

- Each bundle is then given a title or label.

- Bundles can be displayed by pasting words in groups to large charts (or by using pins or removable adhesive so that positions can be easily changed).

- These charts may be added to during the course of the unit.

MODIFICATIONS

- Bundling can be done with individual words, statements, questions or pictures.

- This can be a useful way to lead into statement writing, for example: *Use some of the words in each bundle to make up a sentence about what you know.*

- The lists created through this activity can form the beginnings of vocabulary lists to be drawn on for other language activities throughout a unit.

TEACHING POINTS

- At the tuning-in stage, students may also have very rudimentary, non-technical vocabulary, so the list of words about the topic may be limited. As with all these activities, it is important to accept their offerings at this stage and provide regular opportunities to revisit and make changes.

- Allow initial groupings to emerge rather than pre-determining them. As the unit progresses, more suitable ways of grouping ideas and more technical language for labelling them will develop.

- If this activity is done in groups, it is worthwhile having each group share their bundling decisions with others.

A whole-class 'bundling' of animal words (5–7 year olds)

Chatterboxes

This activity is a fun way of combining a once-popular children's game with some serious thinking!

BASIC PROCEDURE

- Time needs to be set aside to teach students how to make the 'chatterboxes' themselves. For those who don't remember from their own school days, here is a quick reminder!

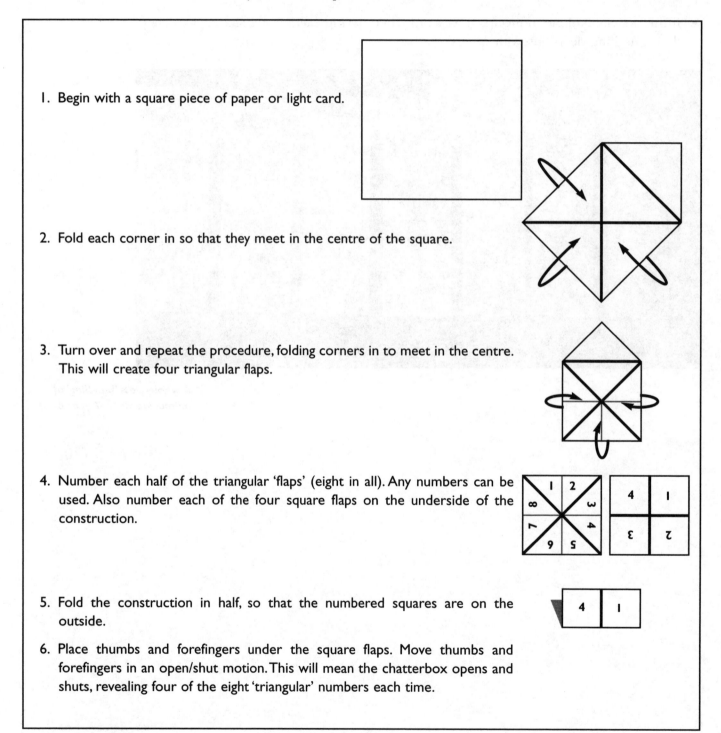

1. Begin with a square piece of paper or light card.

2. Fold each corner in so that they meet in the centre of the square.

3. Turn over and repeat the procedure, folding corners in to meet in the centre. This will create four triangular flaps.

4. Number each half of the triangular 'flaps' (eight in all). Any numbers can be used. Also number each of the four square flaps on the underside of the construction.

5. Fold the construction in half, so that the numbered squares are on the outside.

6. Place thumbs and forefingers under the square flaps. Move thumbs and forefingers in an open/shut motion. This will mean the chatterbox opens and shuts, revealing four of the eight 'triangular' numbers each time.

- Once the chatterboxes have been assembled and numbered, students write a question about the topic underneath each of the eight triangular sections.

- Working in pairs, students play the chatterbox game:

  - Student A holds the chatterbox while their partner (student B) chooses a number on the outside (the square flaps).

  - Student A opens and shuts the chatterbox as many times as the number requires.

  - Next, student B chooses a number from one of the inside, triangular flaps.

  - Again, the chatterbox opens and shuts the required number of times.

  - Finally, student B chooses another number from one of the inside, triangular flaps.

  - This time, the corresponding flap is lifted to reveal a question. Student A asks the question. Student B answers. If they are right, it is their turn to question their partner. If not, they try again.

MODIFICATIONS

- Colors or even topic words can be used instead of numbers. The chatterbox is moved according to the number of letters in the word.

- Instead of questions beneath each flap, answers could be written for which a question must be provided! True and false statements may also be used.

- Questions included under the flaps can be designed to find out students' feelings or opinions about a topic – in which case there is no 'right answer' and the activity becomes more like an interview.

- Chatterboxes can be stored in an area of the classroom and accessed by the students during free time.

TEACHING POINTS

- Squares of 20 x 20 cm make a good size to begin with.

- If students have never made one of these devices, include the activity as a small teaching group during a rotating activity session. This way you will be able to provide 1–1 assistance as it is required.

- If the thought of 27 chatterboxes in the one room is too much, you could begin by making one yourself and having individual students come up to play a quick game with you. This is a good way of introducing the strategy to them.

Cover puzzles

Students try to guess the identity of an image as it is slowly revealed.

BASIC PROCEDURE

- Select a good quality image (eg a poster, large photo or big-book cover). Cover the image with pieces of card (attach with removable adhesive).

- Explain to students that there is a picture beneath the card, and it is their task to try to guess what it is.

- Remove one of the card pieces and ask students to comment on what they see. What could it be?

- Keep removing the card pieces, allowing time for discussion after each one.

- Finally, the full picture is revealed and discussed.

MODIFICATIONS

- A sheet of card can be placed over the picture and small flaps cut in strategic places. The flaps are lifted to reveal parts of the picture (like an advent calender).

- Color transparencies projected onto a screen are a very effective way of conducting this procedure. Simply cover the transparency with pieces of paper and remove one at a time. The image will be easily seen by the class.

TEACHING POINTS

- The most important part of this activity is the discussion that occurs while students are trying to guess the picture. This discussion will often reveal understandings and misconceptions.

- Teacher questioning is critical to the success of the activity. Useful questions include:

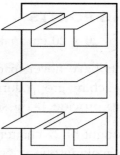

  What does this piece make you think of?
  Why do you think that?
  Why does it remind you of that?
  What else could it be?
  How did you work that out?
  Do you still think it is a ....?
  Why have you changed your mind?

- It is important to accept all suggestions as the picture is revealed. Students should modify their *own* ideas as they gain more information.

- Once the picture has been revealed, it could provide the basis for a picture chat or brainstorm or, if it is the cover of a book, some prediction about the content to follow.

Finish the sentence

In this activity, students are asked to complete sentences about the topic generated by the teacher. In so doing, the students reveal something about their prior knowledge or feelings about the topic.

BASIC PROCEDURE

- Using your unit understandings as a guide, design a set of statement beginnings, for example:

  Rules are important in a community because …
  We know something is a living thing because …

- Students complete the sentence, either verbally, pictorially or in written form.

MODIFICATIONS

- Sentence beginnings can be designed to elicit feelings, opinions or experiences related to the topic, for example:

  A good leader …
  Friends are important to me because …

- Students can work in groups to generate several possible endings to the sentence.

- Provide the whole class with one, open ended sentence beginning and share the diversity of responses. The sentence beginning could be written onto a large sheet of paper and students encouraged to add to it over several days

TEACHING POINTS

- Young students may need to rehearse the conventions of a 'full sentence' before completing the activity.

- Students could keep a record of their sentences to refer back to for self-assessment purposes later in the unit.

Graffiti board

Sheets of paper are placed around the room for students to add words, phrases, pictures etc, as they come to mind. This activity can be carried out during other tasks.

BASIC PROCEDURE

- Display large sheets of paper around the room. In the middle of each sheet, write a key word, phrase or question related to the unit understandings.

- Explain to students that they are free to write or draw any ideas that are sparked by the words displayed. They should write them so they are clear enough for others to read from a distance.

- Leave the sheets up for the first week/s of the unit and encourage students to fill them in in their own time.

- Once sheets have several ideas on them, use the 'print walk' strategy in Chapter 7. Ask students to consider the patterns and connections they see between ideas and to discuss any ideas that interest or baffle them.

MODIFICATIONS

- Graffiti sheets could also have pictures or photographs attached to them.

- They may be left up in the classroom for the duration of the unit. Change the color of the marker used for writing each week to help you see the growth and change in students' ideas.

TEACHING POINTS

- Some students may never get the chance to write on the sheets, as they tend to not finish work early or have much spare time available. Put up a schedule of times over the week when certain students can add to the sheets.

Mind mapping

This is a very useful way to help students organise their ideas about a topic. It can help generate questions and establish misconceptions. It is also a useful gauge of the depth of understanding a student brings to a topic.

BASIC PROCEDURE

- There is no particular procedure for teaching mind maps and the final result is a very individual product. When students are starting out, however, the use of cards can be a helpful technique to help them organise and display their ideas. Once they are more used to the strategy, they can write their ideas directly onto paper.

- Give each student approximately 10 small cards.

- On one card, they write the word/phrase that is the subject for the concept map (eg *water*).

- On the remaining cards, they write/draw other words that they consider to be important in relation to the topic. It is a good idea to do this following a brainstorm.

- On big sheets of paper, the cards are grouped or arranged in a way that makes sense to the student. Place the card with the main word in the centre or at the top of the page.

- Lines and arrows are drawn between the words to show connections.

- Cards can be attached with removable adhesive to make reorganisation easier. Ask students to share maps and see if they can 'read' others.

- Generalisations can then be formed on the basis of the connecting ideas shown on the map.

MODIFICATIONS

- You may wish to provide students with key words or pictures and ask them to make a mind map using those words.

- Y-diagrams or 'tree' charts can also be a useful structure for representing ideas.

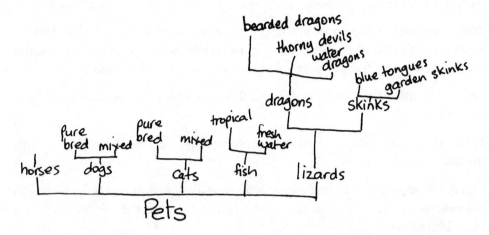

- Students could create a map in pairs or small groups, although this can be difficult in the early stages of a unit where individual understandings may vary enormously.

- Colors can also be used to great advantage in a mind map to help show groupings, connections, priorities, etc.

TEACHING POINTS

- If introducing this strategy to students, work through a mind map as a whole class. Base it on a topic with which the students are very familiar, for example: 'Our school'. Have words and arrows on cards attached to the board with removable adhesive. Students then manipulate the words into position.

- Have some completed mind maps on other topics to show to students. This will help give them an idea of what they are trying to achieve.

- Encourage students to verbalise their maps as they are creating them. This can help them come up with appropriate connecting phrases. Make a list of possible connecting phrases as a resource for students.

- Keep or photocopy initial mind maps as the basis for assessment later in the unit (for example, to be compared with a concept map made later in the unit). Mind maps are an excellent task to repeat at various stages through a unit in order to show growth in understanding.

Mystery boxes

This is an adaptation of the '20 questions' game. It is a great way to introduce a brand new topic to students.

BASIC PROCEDURE

- Choose a set of objects relevant to the topic you are introducing. For example, a shell, sand and dried seaweed for a unit on the marine environment; an apple, a running shoe and a toothbrush for a unit on keeping healthy; a leaf, some soil and a watering can for a unit on plants.

- Place one object in the box without students seeing it. Show the box to students and tell them that they must guess what is inside by asking questions to which there can a only be a 'yes' or 'no' response.

- Give students a limit of 20 questions through which to find the identity of the object.

- Once they have guessed the object correctly, repeat the process with another object.

- Once all objects have been guessed, display them and ask students to suggest what they have in common. You then have the beginnings of a class brainstorm.

MODIFICATIONS

- Depending on the topic being explored, you could use the same idea to create 'feely boxes'. Place an object related to the topic in the box. Students try to guess its identity by reaching in and feeling the object. Encourage them to describe the textures they are feeling and to verbalise their thinking as they try to work out the identity of the object.

- Once a student has guessed the object correctly, they are asked to keep it secret. Others may then direct their questions to that student.

- Place a mystery box (well sealed) in the classroom and display some clues nearby. At the end of day or week, ask students to put forward their ideas (and reasons for them). Reveal the mystery object.

- Once students understand how the activity works, they can create their own mystery boxes about the topic and then play a 20-questions game with other students.

TEACHING POINTS

- The style of questioning required of students in this activity may need to be demonstrated and practised. Students need to develop the skill of asking a closed question – one that requires a yes/no answer. These often begin with phrases such as *Is it …?, Does it …?, Can it …?*

• The questions posed by students will provide you with some information about their prior knowledge and understanding of the topic as well as their skills of reasoning and deduction.

Paired interviews

Students interview each other about their understanding of the topic.

BASIC PROCEDURE

• Explain to the students that they are each going to find out what someone else knows about the topic being investigated.

• As a class, list some questions that students could ask each other. For example, for a unit of work on national parks:

What do you think a national park is?
Can you name any national parks?
Have you ever been to a national park? What was it like?
Why do you think we have national parks?
What do you think we could do to find out more about national parks?
Do you have any other comments to make?

• Organise students into pairs and give each one a time limit to interview their partner. After the first 'round', ask some students to report back to the class on what they have found out about their partners' knowledge of the topic.

• Repeat the procedure, swapping roles.

• Students may report orally or in written form – summarising the main points they gathered from the interview.

MODIFICATIONS

• Use *written conversation* rather than oral language to conduct the interview. Students write to each other as if they were speaking.

• Once students have interviewed each other, pairs join to become a group of four and each student explains their interviewee's ideas to the group.

- Role-play the interviews as a news broadcast and perform them to the class. These could also be taped on audio or video and revisited later in the unit.

TEACHING POINTS

- For young students or those unfamiliar to this technique, use only 2 or 3 questions to begin with.

- Discuss some of the important techniques in interviewing someone else: eye contact, nodding, not interrupting, etc.

- This strategy can be used in conjunctions with 'Concentric circles' (page 138).

Pass the ball

This activity has students thinking on their feet! As the ball is passed to them, they must make a contribution to the group. For some learners, the kinaesthetic demands of throwing and catching the ball help stimulate their thinking and enthusiasm.

BASIC PROCEDURE

- Students stand in a circle.

- The teacher begins by saying the name of a student and throwing the ball to him or her, saying: *Tell us something you know about … [eg pets].*

- The child with the ball makes a statement about what they know. They then choose another student to throw the ball to, and so on.

MODIFICATIONS

- This activity can also be used to promote brainstorming. Students simply offer a word about the topic when the ball is thrown to them.

TEACHING POINTS

- This activity works best after other tuning-in tasks have been completed, as some students can find it a little daunting to suddenly have to think of something to say.

- Students may be given the option to 'pass' if they are having difficulty, and signal when they are ready to put something forward.

- Establish some simple rules such as alternating between girls and boys, all statements to be initially accepted and analysed later, only the person with the ball is allowed to speak.

People bingo

This activity is similar to paired interviews in that the focus is on students gathering prior knowledge from each other. It is an effective way to encourage interaction across all the students in the class and helps develop a sense of community.

BASIC PROCEDURE

- Draw up a sheet on which there are several boxes. In each box, write a sentence beginning with the phrase, *Find someone who ...,* for example: *Find someone who knows one way we can reduce pollution* or *Find someone who can speak two languages.* Design the sentences with the purpose of gathering information about prior knowledge or experience about the topic. *Blackline master 1* is provided for this purpose.

- If someone knows the answer to one of the questions, they sign their name in the box. Students move around the room and collect a different signature in each box. Encourage students to talk with each other as they go. They should hear the response from others, not just collect signatures.

- Stop the activity once most sheets are completed and seat everyone in a circle.

- Ask students to introduce others to the group by way of the information they found out about them.

MODIFICATIONS

- If working with beginning readers, you may wish to limit the number of questions to six.

- Use picture prompts to help students read the question and go through the sheet carefully before starting.

- Older students could design their own bingo sheets.

TEACHING POINTS

- Be careful that this does not become a competition for the most signatures, as this defeats the purpose of the activity.

- Reflect on the activity and note those students who have very few signatures. Did they, in fact, spend all their time helping others? Who finished quickly? Why?

- Information from the sheets could be used to develop a profile of each student in relation to that topic.

Picture priorities

Visual images are used to encourage students to consider what they know or how they feel about a topic. Pictures are ranked according to their perceived importance, or sequenced in a way that makes sense to the students, for example: sequencing pictures of an animal's life cycle, or prioritising pictures of women in various roles.

BASIC PROCEDURE

- Collect some pictures that relate to your topic. Old calenders and magazines are a good source. Some commercial picture sets are also available.

- Number each picture, randomly, and display them to students. Allow plenty of time for students to examine the pictures closely.

- Now ask students to rank the pictures in order of their importance, or to sequence them in a way that makes sense to them. (The instruction you give will depend on your topic and your teaching intention.)

- Students record the numbers in their preferred order.

- In small groups, results are shared and compared

- Students may be given a second opportunity to order the pictures.

MODIFICATIONS

- Give a set of pictures to small groups. They must come to a consensus about how they will organise them.

- You could ask students to add their own images to the set of pictures

TEACHING POINTS

- This activity can often provide an indication of the values and attitudes students bring to a topic. Visual images often evoke stronger reactions than the written word.

- Encourage students to verbalise their thinking as they engage in the activity. Prompt them with questions such as:

  Why did you place the picture in this position?
  How does that picture make you feel?
  What does that picture tell you?
  Are there any pictures that don't make much sense to you? Why?

Possible sentences

Words are selected from an unread text. Students must place the word in a sentence. This is an excellent way to tune students into a text and to prepare them to focus on the information. (Adapted from Hornsby, Parry & Sukarna 1992)

BASIC PROCEDURE

- Choose a text that supports the understandings you have planned for the unit. Big books work well with this activity.

- Select some key words from the text. The words should represent aspects of the topic which you would like students to explore.

- Show students the cover of the book and, if appropriate, read them the blurb so they have some idea about the content. Discuss the possible content of the book. This will help students to get a sense of the form of writing used.

- Ask the students to write each word into a 'possible' sentence – as it might appear in the text.

- Once this has been done, students should share their ideas and discuss the similarities and differences between their proposed sentences.

- Now read through the text. Encourage students to think about the extent to which the *meaning* of their sentences matches that of the text.

- Give students the opportunity to revise their sentences if required. Sentences do not have to be the same as those in the text, but the meaning of the key word should be consistent.

MODIFICATIONS

- The activity can be carried out orally. This may be more appropriate for beginning readers and writers, or for students with a non-English speaking background. Working in pairs or small groups also provides support for students in these circumstances.

- This activity can be carried out as a preparation for watching a film or video. Select some key words from the commentary and ask students to put them in sentences they might hear when they watch the video. These can be shared orally or written down.

- Students could work in groups to devise their possible sentences. Give each group a different word from the text.

- You could ask students to consult a dictionary after they have attempted the sentence and before they view the text.

TEACHING POINTS

- If introducing this activity for the first time, work with small groups of students.

- When selecting the words, include some that you think will be familiar to most students. This will boost confidence and help students to engage in the activity.

- This activity is an excellent vehicle for developing prediction and confirmation skills.

Post-a-question

The 'gimmick' of post boxes provides the stimulus for students to write their questions about a topic. As the questions are anonymous, some students may feel less inhibited about the task.

BASIC PROCEDURE

- Ask students to write down questions they have about a topic onto strips of paper.

- These questions are then posted into a 'question box' over the course of, say, the first week of a unit.

- The box is cleared at the end of the week and the questions are classified and displayed under headings.

MODIFICATIONS

- Provide several boxes – each linked to one broad aspect of the topic. Students place a question in each box.

- Put the questions back in the box at the end of the unit and, in the final week, ask students to draw one question out each day and attempt to answer it.

TEACHING POINTS

- For younger students, some revision may need to be done about how to structure a question.

- This activity can be a useful way to avoid the problems of peer pressure or embarrassment when exploring sensitive topics. Questions can be anonymous and, if preferred, dealt with orally rather than displayed.

- Question boxes can be available to students throughout a unit of work, and cleared at the end of each week.

- Teachers could add their own questions to the box, to help ensure that particular content is addressed.

Question of the day

The teacher poses a broad question each day to generate thinking about the topic.

BASIC PROCEDURE

* Make a list of open-ended questions related to the topic. Questions should encourage students to begin hypothesising about the topic rather than searching for one correct answer. Effective key questions often begin with *Why* or *How*. Sample questions include:
  (for a unit on special places) *Why do we have national parks?*
  (for a unit on endangered animals) *How can we help protect endangered animals?*
  (for a unit on life cycles) *How do chickens hatch out of their eggs?*
  (for a unit on fitness) *What do we need to do to stay healthy?*

* Display one question each day of the week. Throughout the day, encourage students to spend a few moments thinking, writing and talking about the question.

* Ask students to take the day's question home and talk with their family about it.

* Use the question as the basis for morning discussion the following day.

MODIFICATIONS

* Choose the daily question from a list generated by the students.

* Make the daily question a focus for brainstorming or 'rocket writing' (writing as much as possible in a given amount of time).

TEACHING POINTS

* Use your planned understandings as the basis for these questions. The questions should relate to significant 'big ideas' about the topic.

* Keep the questions displayed around the room throughout the unit.

* Write the questions up on a chart. Cover each one with a strip of card and reveal it at the beginning of each day.

Rocket writing

Students write 'everything they know' about a topic within a short, set time-frame.

BASIC PROCEDURE

* Explain to students that they will be required to write in silence for a short time about a topic or in response to a question. They need to have a pen/pencil and paper ready.

* Provide a topic or focus question – or you may choose to provide more stimulus for writing through a piece of music, a short story, visual images, etc.

- Tell students that the most important thing is what they are writing about and that they can attend to spelling and grammar after they have written.

- Give students a set time (eg 5 minutes) within which they are to write as much as they can in response. This can be 'hammed' up by counting down to a 'rocket launch' (10...9...8...6...) before writing, and calling students in to land at the end of the given time.

- Now give them time to read over what they have written and make changes or corrections.

- Students then choose sections of their 'rocket writing' to read out to each other or to the class.

MODIFICATIONS

- Depending on students' confidence with both writing and the topic, the time provided can be extended.

- The same task can be done with drawing and /or listing words.

TEACHING POINTS

- It is important to present this activity in a positive and enjoyable way so students do not feel under unnecessary pressure as they write.

- Use the activity sparingly so that the 'novelty' of writing in a given time frame is not lost.

- Provide options of listing, point form or drawing to younger students or students who are reluctant writers.

- Rocket writing samples can be useful for assessment purposes – both of content knowledge and of writing development.

- Repeat the activity at the end of the unit and compare pieces.

Silent jigsaw

This activity stimulates thinking through visual images and encourages cooperation.

BASIC PROCEDURE

- Gather some pictures related to the topic being explored. Paste each to some light card.

- Cut each picture up into several, irregular pieces.

- Organise students into groups of three, facing each other.

- Each child in the group receives a set of mixed picture pieces – students should have portions of each other's images.

- The task is for each student to construct their picture ... in silence!

- This will mean that students will need to give and receive picture pieces to and from each other until each picture is formed.

- Once the pictures have been formed, they can be used as the basis for discussion, comparison, brainstorming, or a picture priorities activity.

MODIFICATIONS

- The same task can also be done with words or sentences written onto cards and then cut up. Each student in the group has a portion of a statement or question about the topic.

TEACHING POINTS

- Make sure the pictures are pasted onto the same colored card and are similar in style – otherwise the task is too simple.

- Use the opportunity not only to discuss the content of the pictures but also the process students went through in order to construct their own images. As the activity is carried out in silence, it requires the use of non-verbal communication skills.

Something from home

This strategy can be put into place before a unit has actually begun. It can be a useful way to engage both students and parents in the next integrated unit topic.

A display of items brought from home for a unit of work about cultural diversity.

BASIC PROCEDURE

- The procedure is simple and will depend largely on the topic being explored. Explain to students what the next topic of study is to be.

- Ask students to think about any items, books, photographs, etc they may have at home that could help the class find out more about the topic.

- As a shared writing activity, construct a letter to parents to explain the topic under investigation and request any relevant items, ideas or information.

- Set up an area in the classroom for the display or storage of resources for the unit. Include time for students to share some of the things they have brought along.

MODIFICATIONS

- Teachers could also include in the letter to parents, a list of the understandings to be developed in the unit and an outline of some of the activities in which students will be engaged.

TEACHING POINTS

- Encouraging students to seek out relevant resources at home means that parents might become more informed and interested about the current class investigation.

- This activity is intended to help students make connections between the ideas they are exploring at school with their 'real' life beyond school.

Startling statements

This is a fun way to get the ball rolling in a unit. It also gives some idea of students' background knowledge.

BASIC PROCEDURE

- Compile a list of startling statements or fascinating facts about the topic to be explored.

- As a quick game, read the statements to students – deleting some of the information.

- Students complete the statements individually.

- Results are shared and compared against the original statements.

MODIFICATIONS

- Startling statements can also be used as the basis for a true–false quiz. Add some statements of your own.

- The activity could be conducted using a quiz-show format. Give students a time limit to complete the statements and add up their final score of correct statements.

TEACHING POINTS

- The use of startling statements is designed primarily to engage students in the topic. They are particularly suitable for middle- to upper-primary students.

- The students' responses can provide some insight into their understanding about various aspects of the topic.

- The activity can be repeated at the end of the unit of work and results compared.

- Make a classroom display of fascinating facts to which students add throughout the unit.

- Useful resources for this activity include the *Guinness Book of Records*, yearbooks, encyclopedias, the Internet.

The question game

This activity is reminiscent of the party game 'Build a story'. Questions are passed around to each group, gradually building up a series of responses.

BASIC PROCEDURE

- Organise students into groups of three or four. Give each group a number, and display the number in the centre of their table.

- Prepare a list of key questions about the topic. The activity will work best if the number of questions matches the number of groups. So, if there are six groups of students, prepare six questions.

- Write each question on the *bottom* of a sheet of paper.

- Distribute the sheets among the groups – one to each.

- Within a given time limit, each group discusses and then records a response to their question at the *top* of the sheet. The top of the sheet is now folded over to hide the response.

- On a given signal, each group passes their sheet on to the next. (This is easy if group numbers are displayed.)

- The procedure is repeated until each group has responded to every question. The sheets are folded down each time so all responses are hidden.

- Once all questions have been responded to, sheets are passed back to the original group.

- That group unfolds the sheet and reads through the various responses. They can choose the one they think best answers the question, or they might write a new response based on the information they now have. Alternatively, they could simply report the responses to the class – commenting on corresponding or conflicting ideas in the collection of responses.

MODIFICATIONS

- This activity could be carried out with one small group. Each student begins with a question, then responds, folds and passes it on to the next.

- Students could draw their responses rather than write them. As they do not see each other's work, the drawings make for interesting comparisons.

- The same activity can be carried out without covering the responses. Each group reads the previous response and considers ideas that could be added or changed.

TEACHING POINTS

- If students are writing a response to the question, you will need to emphasise the importance of clear handwriting and spelling, as others will need to read their work. The group should be encouraged to 'coach' their scribe accordingly.

- This strategy could be used as the basis of a prediction task, with each group responding to a different question about an experience to follow.

- The discussion each group undertakes in responding to a question can provide a useful context for assessment and observation.

Think, pair, share

This strategy provides a useful structure for moving from individual thought to sharing ideas. It encourages all students to participate.

BASIC PROCEDURE

- Pose a question or problem to students and give them a set time to think about their own response. They can use this time to make some jottings, to draw or just to think.

- Students now form pairs and discuss their ideas with each other. Again, a written or drawn record of their ideas can be recorded with an emphasis on coming to some agreement about their ideas.

- After a given time, call students together again and ask various pairs to share their ideas with the rest of the class.

MODIFICATIONS

- The 'share' time could be between two or three pairs rather than the whole class.

- Small booklets could be made for keeping records of each stage of the process – similar to those used for 'Think, wink and decide'.

TEACHING POINTS

- This strategy can be used in a quick and informal way when students are gathered together on the floor. Before a class discussion, they are given a minute to think, two minutes to pair and then the class begins their share time.

• If extending this activity over a longer time-frame, students should keep records of their individual ideas. This can be a useful reference point for assessment later in the unit.

• If the activity is used regularly, make sure students pair with a range of partners.

Children work in pairs, sharing their ideas (6-year-olds).

Think, wink, decide

This is a useful structure to help students generate questions or statements about a topic. (Adapted from Sukarna, Hornsby & Jennings 1996.)

BASIC PROCEDURE

• Give each child a piece of paper which they fold in half to form a booklet.

• On the front page of their 'booklet' they write the topic word, eg *Deserts*. On the next page they write the word *think*, on the next, *wink* and on the next *decide*.

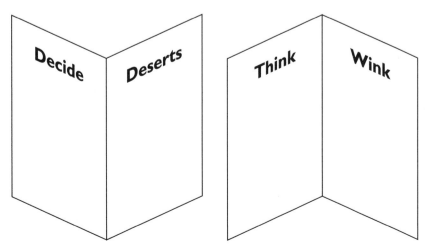

- Students are then given a time limit to do the following on each page:

  Think (**th**ings **I n**ow **k**now) – write down what you already think about the topic.

  Wink (**w**hat **I n**eed to **k**now) – Write down some questions you have about the topic.

  Decide – Select two questions to share with the class.

MODIFICATIONS

- The 'decide' page could also be used to list some ways in which students think they might be able to find out more about the topic.

- The 'decide' page could list questions that a group of students agree on after sharing their 'wink' pages.

TEACHING POINTS

- This activity can provide a useful individual record of prior knowledge.

- Students' ideas could be combined to create a large whole-class version of statements, questions and ways to find out.

Topic wheels

Students fill in their ideas about a topic onto a prepared 'wheel' shape.

BASIC PROCEDURE

- Provide each student or group of students with a blank 'wheel' divided into four sections. (See *Blackline master 2.*) Each section requires students to consider a different aspect of the topic. Instructions can be generic, or specific to the topic.

  Generic topic wheel
  Things I know about this topic
  Things I feel about this topic
  Things I would like to find out about the topic
  Ways I could find out more about the topic

  Specific topic wheel for topic on endangered animals
  Animals I think are endangered
  Animals I think are not endangered
  Causes of endangerment
  Things we can do to protect endangered animals

- Students complete the topic wheels and share. Question marks can be put against the items about which they are less sure.

MODIFICATIONS

- Drawings may be a more appropriate way to fill in the topic wheels.

- A giant topic wheel can be set up on the classroom wall. Students write or draw ideas onto card and pin them to the wheel. This way, the wheel can be modified throughout the unit as more information is gathered.

TEACHING POINTS

- If using the topic wheel as an individual activity, students should keep a copy of their work to revisit later in the unit.

Visualisation and prediction

Prediction is a very effective way of ascertaining the ideas which students bring to a new experience. By making explicit predictions about an event, students are often more focused and engaged in gathering information.

Labelled drawings to show a child's initial understanding of how a torch works.

HOW A TORCH WORKS

When you prees the swech.. The Swech goes back and knockes the batrey and the batrey hits the spring and that pushes the batres to the light

BASIC PROCEDURE

- The procedure used in making predictions will depend on the nature of the event to follow. In order to establish a procedure, first consider what activities you have planned to help students gather new information about the topic.

- Predictions can be carried out before a visit from a guest speaker, an excursion out of school, a film or video, science experiments, having a plant or animal in the classroom, surveys or interviews. (See 'Finding out'.)

- If using predictions to establish prior knowledge, you need to consider what information you would like students to focus on during the experience. Use this as a guide to designing the prediction task.

- Once a structure for the prediction activity has been established, encourage students to 'visualise' their response before they begin representing it. You might say to students, for example:

I want you to close your eyes and see yourself at the farm. Imagine you are stepping off the bus. What is the first thing you see? Take a walk around the farm. What colors can you see? Are there people there? What are they doing? What can you smell? What is the ground like beneath you feet? What sorts of buildings can you see?

Students are now ready to represent their predictions in some way. *Blackline master 3* can be used to record predictions.

MODIFICATIONS

Here are some examples of specific prediction activities related to various topics:

- Students rule up two columns, labelled *guess* and *check*. Ideas are recorded before and confirmed or changed after the experience.

- Provide students with a piece of card that is postcard size. Ask them to design a photograph that might be taken during their outing.

- Before a walk to examine the housing in the local area, students are provided with the outline of the route they will take: *Draw some of the houses you think you might see on this walk.*

- Before an experiment to test objects that float and sink: *Draw a picture to show the objects you think will float and those you think will sink under the water.*

Five-year-olds predict the outcomes of various experiments with water.

I think little black things will come out of the tap water.

The pond water will clear 1st, then the horse droppings, then the grass.

I think the filter paper will go all scungy and soggy.

I think the filter paper will get wet and the water will make a hole to go through.

- Before sharing a story, read students the first few pages and ask them to *continue to tell the story* as they think it will unfold.

- Before having a guest speaker to talk to students, *role-play* an interview between the guest speaker and a class member.

- Before going to the zoo to observe animals, ask students to *show* the way they think the animals will move and what they think they will look and sound like.

TEACHING POINTS

- It is important to accept all predictions. Students will have opportunities to confirm or correct their predictions after the experience.

- More information can be gained by asking students *why* they have made particular predictions. Encourage students to provide a reason for their predictions: *I think we will see … because …*

- Keep a record of some of students' predictions to assist in questioning during an excursion. For example: *Here is the lion enclosure. How similar is this habitat to the one you imagined?*

Visual representation

Drawings, paintings, diagrams and other visual art work can be an excellent vehicle for tuning in and ascertaining prior knowledge about a topic. Many misconceptions are more effectively revealed through drawing.

BASIC PROCEDURE AND MODIFICATIONS

Several of the activities listed in this section lend themselves to visual as well as written or verbal responses. Further ideas for visual representation include:

- *Labelled diagrams* to show students' understanding of how something works or moves or what parts it has
  For example, for a technology unit on transport, students draw and label the parts of a bike and attempt to show how it moves.

- *Comic strips* showing a sequence of events related to a topic
  For example, for a unit on families, students prepare comic strips to illustrate their ideas about the way family members relate to each other.

- *Plasticine models* to represent understanding of how something looks
  For example, for a unit on 'the body' students use plasticine to make models of various parts of the body and where they think those parts are located.

- *Collages* of magazine pictures to represent images relevant to the topic
  For example, for a unit of work on food, students cut out pictures of food they consider to be part of a healthy diet.

- *3D models* using a variety of materials. Models can be set up early in the unit and modified as more information is gathered
  For example, for a unit of work on early Australia, students make a model of how they think the goldfields might have looked.

- *Maps/floor plans* – representing the geography of an area
  For example, for a unit of work on deserts, students mark in on an outline of a world map where they think deserts are. Or they could draw their own map.

- *Flow diagrams* to show the sequence of how something might be made, constructed, grown or changed
  For example, for a unit of work on 'shopping' students design a flow chart to show the process they think occurs in bringing the item to the supermarket.

- *Cut-away or X-ray diagrams* to show how something works or what is inside
  For example, for a unit of work on trees, students draw a cut-away picture of what is inside the trunk.

A 5-year-old uses colored paper to represent her image of a mouse at the beginning of a unit on pets.

I would like a mouse as a pet.
Sally

TEACHING POINTS

- Tuning in through visual art should be a regular part of your integrated program. If you have an art specialist in the school, these activities could be combined with specific skill development and actually carried out in the art room.

- When responding to art works in the context of a unit of work, always begin by responding to the information portrayed by the piece, then move to a discussion of the techniques used to display the information.

- Art work provides an excellent source of assessment and self-assessment. Work produced by students early in the unit can be retained and revisited later in the unit.

- When displaying the art works produced, be explicit about their purpose. Accompany such displays with a sign: *These diagrams show our ideas about how chickens might hatch out of eggs.*

Year 2 students represent their ideas about Australian animals using plasticine.

Word association and definitions

This strategy provides a quick overview of students' familiarity with key topic vocabulary.

BASIC PROCEDURE

- Select a set of key words about the topic you are exploring.

- Words could be written on cards, on the board or on large sheets of butchers' paper.

- Ask students to (i) suggest definitions for the words, (ii) put the words into a sentence, or (iii) write or draw anything that comes to mind when they see or hear these words.

MODIFICATIONS

- This activity can be most effective when combined with 1–3–6 consensus grouping (see page 104).

- Use the activity as the basis for a large class chart of initial definitions with students' names written beside their own definition.

- Students can use a dictionary once they have attempted their own definition.

TEACHING POINTS

- Try to include some familiar words in the list to boost confidence and help 'get the ball rolling'.

- If students are experiencing difficulties, try these prompts:

  What does the word remind you of?
  Do any pictures come to mind when you hear the word?
  Does this word remind you of any other words?

- Keep a record of these initial definitions and encourage students to continually refine their ideas as the unit unfolds.

Five-year-olds attempt a definition of pets.

A pet is an animal that I can take care of? (Lynette)

A Pet is an animal that comes from different places. (Whitney)

Pets are for feeding. (Jason)

You look after pets. (Nathan)

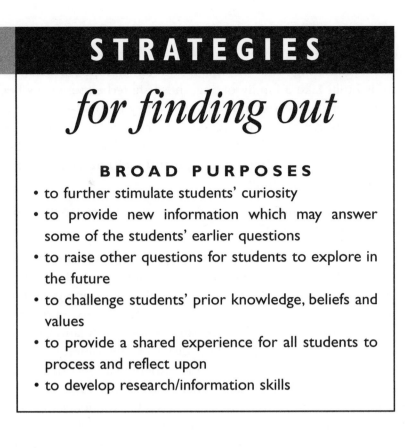

STRATEGIES
for finding out

2

BROAD PURPOSES

- to further stimulate students' curiosity
- to provide new information which may answer some of the students' earlier questions
- to raise other questions for students to explore in the future
- to challenge students' prior knowledge, beliefs and values
- to provide a shared experience for all students to process and reflect upon
- to develop research/information skills

About this stage of a unit

Once students have identified questions, issues and interests related to a topic, they need access to experiences and resources that will provide them with *new* information. It is this information that forms the basis of activities to follow – in mathematics, language, drama, art, music and so on. By providing rich, shared experiences, we give students opportunities to construct concepts and understandings that we, as adults, may take for granted.

Over the course of a year, it is vital to provide students with opportunities to gather new information in a range of ways and from a range of sources. It is argued that a well-constructed program should include a balance of modes of learning (Bruner 1960). The strategies presented at this stage of the unit include experiences which focus on the enactive mode (learning through doing); the iconic mode (through observation); and the symbolic model (through verbal and written symbols – for example by reading or listening to a guest speaker).

Each of the finding-out strategies in this chapter requires students to apply specific skills in gathering and recording data about the topic. It is at this stage where such 'information skills' are highlighted and where students learn to identify the strengths and weaknesses of various data sources and to 'match' a topic of investigation with an appropriate data source.

While some of the strategies presented here can be carried out by individuals, the emphasis is on *whole-class* activity. As students share in the experience of gathering new information *about* a topic, a sense of class community is built. Like a family outing, these shared experiences become a reference point for discussion and reflection. They help to focus the class on their shared investigation. It is argued by proponents of philosophy for children, in particular, that children's thinking is enhanced when they learn to 'inquire together'. Cam (1995) and Lipman (1988) argue for inquiry as a 'social practice' in the classroom:

> If we want children to think for themselves, we should engage them in thinking toegether. (Cam 1995, p. 17)

While these writers are referring to a community of inquiry developed around philosophical discussion, the same can be said of the shared experiences students undertake during an inquiry-based integrated unit. The interaction between learners both during and after the experiences is often critical to the interpretation and processing of the information gathered. By experiencing the event together, they discover the different perspectives through which individuals view the same experience, and they are able to 'test' their responses out on each other and to fill gaps in memory or oversights in observation. Naturally, sharing such experiences also provides opportunities for students to develop important social skills such as turn-taking; acknowledging different points of view, and sharing resources.

The teachers' role at the finding-out stage undergoes an important shift. Where, at tuning in, the role was one of observation, listening, analysis and recording, the emphasis is now on challenging and extending students' understandings. Much of the time, the texts and experiences themselves 'do the teaching' but it is the teacher's skilled selection and management of these resources that enables this extension to take place. Informed by the planned understandings for the unit, the teacher seeks 'teachable moments' during the finding-out stage – probing with questions; alerting students to observe particular features or events; revising key information; and explaining and linking new experiences with previous predictions or questions.

The following list is not exhaustive. Provided are the most common ways of accessing information, together with some ideas for making the most of the experience. These activities are best preceded by one or more of the tuning-in tasks outlined in the previous section. If students are tuned in to the experience, they are likely to focus on more than just the bus trip!

Animals and plants in the classroom

For units of work dealing with the growth, development and characteristics of living things, bringing animals or plants into the classroom can be a wonderful shared experience and the basis for some excellent cross-curriculum responses.

ADVANTAGES

- Activities such as designing and building an enclosure, researching the food requirements, setting up monitoring systems, observing, monitoring, measuring and recording all provide excellent opportunities for teaching and learning in a wide range of areas.

- Living things in the classroom provide an ongoing source of first-hand data.

- Caring for animals and plants can develop positive attitudes, a sense of responsibility, an understanding of a range of values about animals and a heightened feeling of class community.

USEFUL SOURCES

- Each department of education may have their own regulations about animals, in particular, that can be kept in the classroom. Similarly, departments of wildlife or conservation may also have guidelines that restrict the keeping of certain species. It is important to check with the relevant authorities. Some animals might be sold in pet shops but may, in fact, require licences or permits to be kept.

- There are only some varieties of plants and animals suitable for keeping in classroom environments. Whichever you choose, their presence in the classroom should be regarded as short-term, and thorough knowledge of their care requirements should be gained beforehand. The following animals may be suitable for classroom observation:

  - small rodents (mice, rabbits, guinea pigs, hamsters, gerbils)
  - invertebrates (earthworms, ants, snails, slaters, mealworms, crickets, caterpillars and butterflies)
  - amphibians (common species of tadpoles and frogs, axolotl)
  - birds (juvenile chickens, ducks, quail)
  - reptiles (common small lizards and small non-venomous snakes – although permits are definitely required for these)
  - fish (common fresh-water varieties)

- If growing plants in the classroom or school ground, contact a local nursery to find out about species that are indigenous to the area. They will be more likely to grow successfully and will help create a more appropriate habitat for animals. Check that indoor plants are suited to the conditions of your classroom.

TEACHING POINTS

- The most important aspect of this particular shared experience is that students play an active role in the preparation and care for the living things. Rather than bring a plant or animal into the classroom unannounced, use tuning-in strategies to help students predict and prepare for their arrival.

- To assist in gathering data about the living things, systems need to be organised for timing and recording observations. Diaries, charts, cameras and tape recorders should all be accessible, and rosters need to be set up for data collection, cleaning and feeding. The handling of animals needs to be given careful thought. Some teachers have a box of disposable gloves for students to wear. All students and teachers should be instructed on the safest and least harmful way to handle any animal.

- Animals need to be housed in a quiet area of the room with some part of their enclosure screened.

- Keeping animals in the classroom requires time, skill and, often, money! You may have a willing parent who might help build a suitable enclosure, care for the animals at the weekend or even offer them a home at the end of the unit. All this should be investigated early on.

Year 2 students observe a mouse to find out more about living things.

Ask an expert

Inviting an expert to the classroom can be an excellent way to gather information as well as developing the skills of listening, speaking, questioning and recalling.

ADVANTAGES OF GUEST SPEAKERS AS A SOURCE OF INFORMATION

- Experts in a field are often passionate about their topic. This enthusiasm can be motivating for students.

- Feelings and values associated with the topic will emerge through discussion with people more so than by reading books or even watching video or film.

- Students have the opportunity to ask specific, direct questions.

USEFUL SOURCES OF GUEST SPEAKERS

- Parents and grandparents of the students themselves. You will have many experts in a wide range of fields at your fingertips.

- Members of local community groups – historical societies, conservation groups, cultural groups.

- Some education departments publish lists of organisations that make speakers available to school groups.

TEACHING POINTS

It is important to prepare thoroughly for the visit.

- Talk to the guest speaker before they visit the class. Even if they are familiar with speaking to school students, they should be aware of the focus of your students' investigations. Send them a copy of the understandings around which your unit is based and of any questions the students have raised so far.

- Ask the guest speaker, if possible, to bring some concrete artefacts with them. This is a useful focus for students and helps them recall information more effectively.

- If more than one guest speaker is attending, consider grouping the students and rotating speakers around the groups. Smaller groups may mean more interaction.

- Be clear about the time the speaker has available. Keep it short – some speakers are less familiar with the attention span of a young audience.

- Construct a list of questions for the guest speaker before they arrive. Not only is this a good way to find out more about the knowledge students bring to a topic, it will be a prompt during the discussion.

- 'Rehearse' the visit prior to the guest's arrival. Who will ask the questions? How will we thank the guest speaker? Also remind students of the importance of their 'body language' when listening to a guest speaker – eye contact, etc. Consider the seating arrangements. Ensure all students can see and hear adequately and that the speaker can be comfortably seated.

- Consider how the information provided by the speaker will be recorded. It may be useful to make a video or audio tape of the interview that could be revisited later in the unit to check information. Students may also make some jottings during the interview – although this can distract them from actually listening to the information.

- Take some photos of your visitor working with the students to add to class records of the unit or to accompany reports, and so on (see 'Sorting out').

- Letters of thanks – focusing on what was learned from the visitor – are a useful follow-up and help to reinforce the information gathered.

CD-ROMs

CD-ROMs can be a wonderful resource for teachers as well as students. The speedy access to information is a great support in the unit-planning process as teachers develop their own background knowledge about a topic.

ADVANTAGES

- The technology is generally very easy to use and can often be accessed independently by students.

- Like books and videos, they can be revisited.

- Information can be located quickly, skipped and returned to.

- Unlike the Internet, a CD is dedicated to a specific topic. Search time is not wasted.

- For students who lack confidence in reading, many CDs provide easy pathways to information, combining written instructions with common computer tools (clicking buttons, etc).

- CDs are a useful way to learn certain research skills such as using key words to locate information.

- The combination, in many CDs, of sound, vision, written text and interactive activities can be very engaging for learners.

- Like most computer-based technologies, the experience is generally best suited to individuals or pairs.

SOURCES

- School, community and university libraries are building up collections of CDs. At the time of writing, they were still a relatively expensive resource. Sharing between schools is encouraged.

- More and more suitable CDs are coming on to the market. Some general knowledge CDs that can be used for a range of units include:

  The Oxford Children's Encyclopaedia on CD-ROM, Dorling Kindersley Multimedia, 1996.
  World Book Multimedia Encyclopaedia, 1996.

- Several newspapers (eg the Melbourne *Age*) have also compiled CD-ROMs which store hundreds of articles and can be searched by topic.

Using a CD-ROM to gather information.

TEACHING POINTS

- Small groups of students can work with a CD while other students are engaged in other activities.

- A CD that deals with your topic can be made available to students *throughout* the unit of work.

- Opt for the more interactive CDs that encourage problem-solving.

- Screen the CDs carefully before purchase. The quality of information varies enormously. It is important that students are gathering worthwhile data and that it is not obscured by the 'bells and whistles' in the production.

Excursions

Visiting places away from school can be a powerful form of shared experience. The opportunity for students to experience a new environment and to gather information first-hand usually creates a lasting impression and provides wonderful 'fodder' for cross-curriculum responses to follow.

ADVANTAGES

- Visiting a site associated with your topic will often provide far richer information than students can access through books or video. This is the real thing.

SOURCES

- Many education departments publish lists of excursion venues suitable for schools.

- A staff brainstorm of successful venues at the beginning of the year is a good way to share past experiences with each other. Also invite parents to suggest places they may know of in the local community. The general list provided below may spark some ideas for particular excursions in your area:

airports	local, state and national parks
bakeries	markets
cemeteries	museums
community services — police department, fire department, post office, hospital	newspaper offices
	outdoor environment — coast, forest, rivers, lakes, etc.
construction sites	ruins
displays of various collections	school camping venues
dockyards	special interactive exhibits on particular topics
factories	
farms	theatres — including behind-the-scenes tours
galleries	
government offices	TV stations
historical sites	universities
libraries	workshops or artist studios
local shopping centres	zoos

- Several venues have a home page on the Internet that will provide information on cost, bookings, and so on.

Using the outdoors to gather direct information about plants.

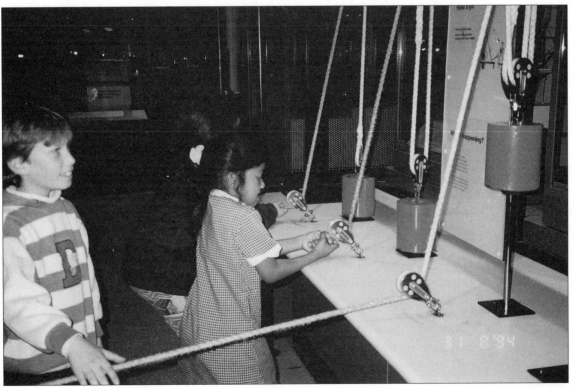

Seven-year-olds gather information about machines at a science museum.

TEACHING POINTS

- The key to a successful excursion is preparation – both practical and intellectual. The prediction strategies suggested in the tuning-in section are useful ways to prepare students to gather information. Students should undertake their visit with at least one key question in mind.

- Young students may benefit from writing their question on, say, the back of their name tag. This will provide you or parent leaders with a focus for discussion.

- Consider efficient ways to record data during your excursion. Cameras are a must, and small tape recorders (to record quick, on-the-spot interviews or observations), notepads, sketch pads and prepared checklists are all useful tools for gathering and recording data. Make sure students know what their observation task is before they arrive at the site.

- An excursion provides you with an excellent opportunity to explicitly work with the prior knowledge assessed during the tuning-in stage.

- Where possible, organise students into small groups with parent leaders. This will enable greater questioning and interaction during the visit. Meet with leaders before the excursion to discuss the purpose of the excursion and the information you hope students will gain from it.

- Take a small notebook with you to record ideas for sorting-out activities as they arise during the excursion.

Experiments

Experiments can be loosely defined as activities in which students engage to explore a particular (often physical) phenomenon. This may be as simple as working out which materials float or sink, or as complex as designing a model volcano.

ADVANTAGES

- Experiments should be hands on, interactive experiences in which students are actively involved, rather than passive observers. This active involvement usually means a high level of engagement in learning. It provides an opportunity for students to construct for themselves what may be a taken-for-granted concept for adults.

- Hands-on experiments help to develop important skills of prediction, organisation, team work, observation, record-keeping and, importantly, problem-solving.

- Some experiments can be repeated during the course of the unit to compare or revise results. Information is immediate and first hand.

SOURCES

- Hands-on experiments are usually most relevant to science and technology based topics. There is a rich variety of resource material specific to these curriculum areas in which the procedures for such activities are outlined.

- Also consider faculties of science and technology at local universities and colleges (some have centres specifically designed for working with younger students or may be willing to assist with equipment).

- Teaming up with a neighboring high school is often a good way to access equipment and expertise.

- The relevant subject associations in your state may be a good starting point for ideas.

TEACHING POINTS

- Hands-on experiments are too often experienced by students as fun but isolated, one-off activities. Experiments should be planned as a part of a broader, integrative unit. It is important that students can place the activity within a broader framework of meaning.

- Pairs or small groups are usually the best set-up for experiments – for both safety and effective learning.

- The skills of cooperative learning are often needed in these activities. Make sure students are clear about their roles.

- Consider working with each group as a teaching group throughout the week rather than having the whole class involved in the same activity. This can save on materials, stress and mess!

Film, video and television

These are media with which almost all students are very familiar. As a visual text, video provides students with sound and images to engage them in a topic.

ADVANTAGES

- Video is an excellent way for students to gather information about subjects they cannot experience directly.

- Through video, students can experience powerful visual images that help form the basis of creative responses and explorations later in the unit.

- Videos can be reviewed, revisited, used in sections or viewed again by individuals or small groups.

SOURCES

- Several educational departments have film and video libraries. Ask for a catalogue. University, college and local libraries are another useful source. Be on the look-out for documentaries and other television programs that might be relevant to topics you are exploring. A weekly look through the television guide with students is worth the time.

TEACHING POINTS

- Use some tuning-in strategies to prepare specifically for the video. These might include: oral possible sentences, prediction and listing key questions.

- You could allocate groups of students to keep notes about particular aspects or sections of the video.

- Consider watching the video – or part of it – with the sound turned down. This enables questioning and discussion and may mean that the information is more accessible to young students.

- It can be very effective to pause the video regularly to check for understanding, ask for feedback, pose a question for the next section, and so on.

Interviews and surveys

Like guest speakers, interviews and surveys are useful ways in which students can gather first-hand information, ideas, feelings and opinions. Interviews develop confidence and skills in questioning, listening, recording and recalling. Surveys provide concrete data for processing. This is a useful way to teach students that we can learn much from talking with and listening to others.

ADVANTAGES

- Depending on the topic, students may be able to gather information simply by interviewing or surveying other students, teachers, family and friends. The resources are close at hand.

- If conducting interviews and surveys individually, students have a great deal of responsibility to gather and report on the information.

- If all students conduct just one interview or survey each, the information received is often rich and diverse.

- Interviews and surveys often lead to new pathways for investigation.

- Interviews can be tailored to the interests of each particular child.

SOURCES OF PEOPLE FOR INTERVIEW

(See also guest speakers)

- This will, of course, depend on the topic being investigated. However, many social education topics lend themselves to interviewing family and friends about their experiences, feelings or beliefs. Consider the school community as the first reference point for an interview.

- Surveys can be distributed to a wider audience – not necessarily known to the students. This audience could include parents, teachers and students in the school, local residents, clubs, or students in a nearby school.

Students interviewing each other about their role in families.

TEACHING POINTS

- View and or listen to interviews on radio or television. Discuss some of the techniques used. What makes an interview successful or unsuccessful?

- Check newspapers and magazines for sample survey formats. Make a collection of these to help decide on the best format for your survey.

- Help students prepare a list of questions or survey items.

- Model a sample interview in front of the students, perhaps with another teacher.

- Consider jointly constructing a survey with the students.

- Always make sure that students have a clear understanding of what it is they are trying to find out.

- Rehearse! Once a set of questions has been developed, students should practise asking them of each other. Discuss and rehearse interview protocol:
  - *explaining the purpose of the interview*
  - *seeking permission for the interview to be recorded*
  - *thanking the interviewee*

- Consider ways of recording the interview using video, tape recorder or notes.

- Students could arrange to conduct interviews in pairs – one responsible for questioning, the other for recording.

- Make sure that information gained from the interview or survey is processed quickly (see 'Sorting out') while it is still fresh in the students' minds.

Letter writing

Many organisations or individuals can help provide information to students for their investigations. Writing to those organisations may be a whole-class, group or individual activity. Don't forget the potential of e-mail to speed the process where possible.

ADVANTAGES

- The task of constructing a letter to request information develops important literacy skills and conventions.

- Letters requesting information can be tailored to the specific needs and interests of the individual or class.

- Letters require careful thought and deliberation, and help students to fine tune what it is they wish to find out.

- If thoughtfully written, a letter may be the best way of procuring information from an expert who will appreciate the time and trouble taken by the students.

SOURCES

- Naturally, letters can be written to any organisation or individual; however, some sources will have policies and practices that will determine their response. It is worth finding out prior to writing whether or not the organisation has a policy of responding to letters from schools, and what is the best way to approach them.

- Various organisations such as the local council, education department or subject organisations often publish lists of relevant organisations to whom students may write.

- It is a good idea to keep a copy of the local address directory in the classroom.

TEACHING POINTS

- The success of letters in procuring information often depends on their presentation, accuracy and clarity.

- Model the conventions of letter writing to students. Use this as an opportunity to teach the various conventions associated with letter writing in a meaningful context. You may choose to construct a letter together – writing it on a large chart or overhead projector transparency.

- Letters should be kept concise and to the point. Explain to the organisation what the topic of investigation is, perhaps a little about what you have been investigating so far and, specifically, what kind of information you are looking for.

- You may need to do your letter-writing activities early on in the unit to ensure that information will arrive when you need it!

- Include a stamped and self-addressed envelope with the letter.

- On receiving information, write a short note of thanks, mentioning ways in which the information was useful.

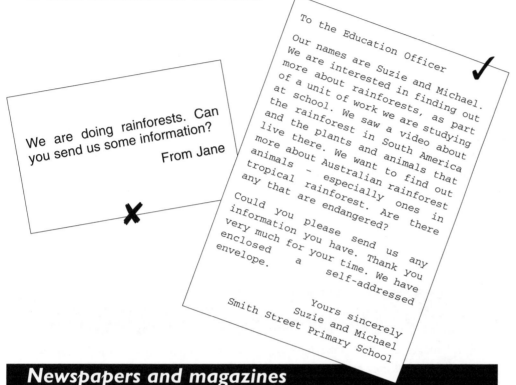

Two contrasting sample letters asking for information.

We are doing rainforests. Can you send us some information?
From Jane

To the Education Officer

Our names are Suzie and Michael. We are interested in finding out more about rainforests, as part of a unit of work we are studying at school. We saw a video about the rainforest in South America and the plants and animals that live there. We want to find out more about Australian rainforest animals – especially ones in tropical rainforest. Are there any that are endangered?

Could you please send us any information you have. Thank you very much for your time. We have enclosed a self-addressed envelope.

Yours sincerely
Suzie and Michael
Smith Street Primary School

Newspapers and magazines

As everyday texts, newspapers and magazines offer a ready source of information to students. Using newspapers is also a useful way to help students develop skills in critical literacy.

ADVANTAGES

- Newspapers, in particular, are often useful sources for investigating current affairs. They provide students with 'real-life' information and can be an important way to link broader concepts being explored with events happening in the local and/or global community.

- The combination of written and visual text in newspapers and magazines provides two different vehicles for gathering information.

- Newspapers will often echo stories students have watched on the news at home and may, therefore, be familiar to them.

- Newspapers and magazines are an easy source of information to obtain.

SOURCES

- Many schools subscribe to a newspaper. You could also consider asking a family to donate copies to your class after they have finished reading. It is worthwhile scanning the local paper for articles relevant to current or future units, as these may have more relevance to your students.

- Keep a file of articles you may use in the future. Encourage older students to check the newspaper for interesting articles or photographs. This may be rostered as part of silent reading time.

TEACHING POINTS

- Many newspaper and magazine articles are too complex for young students to read independently. Structured reading strategies that help prepare for and support the reading process are best used in conjunction with articles. Some of these strategies include possible sentences, directed reading and thinking activities, and cloze.

- If using this strategy as a means through which to gather information, it may be best carried out with a small teaching group.

- Newspapers can be particularly useful as sources of stories for values clarification. As they often report on conflicts or problems arising from various situations, they are an excellent source of ideas for role-play and debate.

- Newspapers and magazines, like video and television, should also be examined for the ways in which they report news – not just the news itself.

Paintings, photographs, drawings and other visual images

Visual images can be a powerful way for students to find out about places, people and events that they cannot experience first hand or that might provide a contrast to their own experience.

ADVANTAGES

- Without written or spoken text to accompany the image, students must rely on their own interpretation. This has the advantage of encouraging discussion, raising points of view and stimulating questions.

- As students live in a world in which they are bombarded with visual imagery, it is important that they are given opportunities to practise critically 'reading' these images and understanding the nature of their response and interpretation.

SOURCES

There are many, many sources of visual images for a wide range of topics. These include:
- photographs and illustrations in books
- commercially produced 'picture sets'
- posters
- copies of paintings and other art works
- photographs and slides
- pictures from magazines and newspapers

TEACHING POINTS

- Visual images can be used both directly and indirectly in an integrated unit.

- They may simply be placed around the room to stimulate thinking and discussion, or they can be used in a more structured way to encourage students to make particular observations. For example, in a unit on insects, an enlarged photograph of an ant will allow students to gather information they would not necessarily gain from observing a real ant.

- Images can be provided to students with a list of broad focus questions to guide their observation.

- Many visual images also lend themselves to discussions about the technique used by the creator of the image. Talk with students about why particular images are powerful, frightening, persuasive, and so on.

- Discuss the messages the image maker wants the 'reader' to take away. Consider how those messages or values may be similar to or different from our own.

- Use the images to encourage students to experiment with their own visual techniques in the sorting-out phase.

Picture books and novels

Picture story books and novels are vital for developing reading skills and providing enjoyment in the classroom. They also offer a powerful source of new ideas, information, experiences and feelings about a wide range of topics.

ADVANTAGES

- Children's literature is a wonderful means by which students can access the experience that others have had of the world.

- Depending on the topic, literature will often provide not only new information to students but raise issues, values and feelings associated with the topic.

- Using literature for this purpose will often help students to make sense of the text in more powerful ways. The literature program is then meaningfully integrated into the curriculum.

SOURCES

- There are several listings of literature under themes or topics. Many teacher reference books focused on literature examine ways in which books can be grouped and used under the umbrella of a common theme. Some recommended titles include:

  V. Nicoll & V. Roberts, *Literature-Based Programs*, PETA, NSW 1993

  M. Dibella & J. Hamston, *Undercover: Exploring Values through Children's Literature*, Collins Dove, Melbourne 1989

  M. Stiller, *The Joy of Children's Books*, Tiltili Books, Port Adelaide 1989

TEACHING POINTS

- There is a wealth of picture story books and novels that can be used in conjunction with integrated units of work. The key to their selection is to ensure that they really support the understandings being taught and are not simply 'about' the topic. For example, Maurice Sendak's *Where the Wild Things Are* is a superb book, but reading it will not help students come to understand more about the differences between wild and domestic animals. This may be a better book to read in the context of a unit of work about relationships or growing up.

- Literature to support the goals of the unit may be explored within the body of a unit itself or as part of the regular literature program.

- Try choosing 4 or 5 titles of various levels of reading difficulty. Allocate these to groups as appropriate and work through the books during the unit of work. Many of the sorting-out activities in the next chapter can be used to help students respond to and work with the text.

Literature used to gather data about housing.

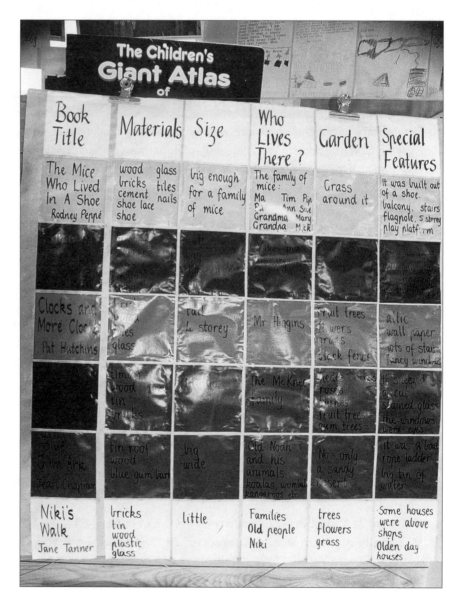

Phone calls

Phone calls can be a quick way to request information or conduct a short interview.

ADVANTAGES

- Phone calls are an excellent way to teach students about the appropriate 'etiquette' when requesting information and to develop confidence, and listening and speaking skills.

- The information is gained on the spot rather than delayed by mail or other, slower, forms of communication.

SOURCES

See guest speakers and excursions, pages 47 and 50.

TEACHING POINTS

- If students are phoning organisations in their own time, ensure that it is in fact the students – not the parents – who make the call. Send a note home to explain the purpose of the activity.

- It is a good idea to *model* a phone request. Show students how to make a polite, specific, informed request.

- Have students role-play conversations in pairs (old phones in the classroom are a useful prop for drama). Include: using the person's name, introducing themselves, naming the school, checking that the listener has time to speak, briefly explaining their request, providing fax number or address, thanking the person for their time, and speaking clearly and sounding enthusiastic.

- Rehearse calls prior to making them. Show students how to make some 'phone notes' to remind them what to say – and also to record information from the speaker.

Shared book experience

This literacy strategy can be adapted for use within an integrated unit of work. It serves as both a reading task and a way of gathering information – as a group – about the topic. A big book or multiple copies of small books are needed.

ADVANTAGES

- Because your are sharing in the reading process, many techniques for reading for meaning can be modelled.

- Books can be revisited throughout a unit to check on or revise information.

- Books may provide a model for ways in which students can write about and illustrate the topic later in the unit.

- Factual texts can be read in sections, ensuring students do not suffer from 'information overload'.

SOURCES

Shared book experiences are generally carried out using a big-book format. Over the last few years, there has been a huge increase in the number of information-based big books published. Many of the large educational publishers are now including factual big books on a range of topics as part of their reading schemes. Some examples include:

Realisation – Rigby
Connections – Macmillan
Voyages – Nelson
Science Alive – Mimosa
Finding Out About ... – Macmillan

A group of independent readers share a big book.

TEACHING POINTS

- Big books dealing with non-fiction topics need to be well prepared for. Some of the tuning-in strategies mentioned in the previous section are particularly appropriate. These include cover puzzles, word association, possible sentences and prediction.

- Show students how the index and contents pages can be used to locate specific information – perhaps those sections that deal with the questions that have arisen in the unit so far.

- An easel or big-book stand and a pointer are useful ways of helping students see the pages clearly. Big books can be very awkward to hold up in front of a class.

- You may wish to add to the intrigue by covering some of the key words in the text and asking students for suggestions as you read. Removable labels are useful for this.

- After you have read the book – or part of it – aloud, make links back to some of the ideas that emerged during the tuning-in activities. The following are useful, general questions to spark discussion:
  What new information did this book give us?
  Are there sections you would like to reread?
  Is there anything that surprised you? Why?
  Has this book answered any of our questions?
  Do you have some new questions now that we have read this book?
  What do you think the author needed to do/know in order to write the book?
  Why do you think the author wrote this book?

- Many big books are packaged with a set of small books. These can be used by individual students for follow-up work.

Structured observations

This is an excellent way for students to gather first-hand data and to teach an important research skill.

ADVANTAGES

- Structured observations develop skills in focusing, gathering data and observing detail.

- The data gathered is usually diverse and teaches students that we each see things differently.

SOURCES

- This depends on the topic being studied. Generally, observations will be most easily conducted in the local environment – the school ground, local shopping centre, park, market, and so on. Structured observations can be used as part of an excursion (see page 50).

- Some examples of units for which structured observations might be used include:
  Family life: observing interactions between family members in a community venue
  Cooperation and competition: observing a sporting event, a group of seagulls, a playground of 5-year-olds
  Transport: observing the various kinds of transport in a particular location
  Animal life: observing the behavior of animals at a zoo or in their natural habitat
  Plant life: regular observations of the growth of a plant, changes in size and appearance, and so on.

TEACHING POINTS

- The word 'structured' is the essence of this strategy. Students need to be clear about why they are observing this particular scene and have an effective means of recording their observations. This should be done prior to visiting the site.

- Prediction (see 'Tuning in') will help focus students on the task and the information they are gathering.

- The record-keeping devices will depend on the kind of data that is being gathered. Photography, video, tape recorders, note-taking, checklists, anecdotal record sheets, tally sheets and sketch pads are all useful devices.

- Observations generally work best if they are short and focused. It is sometimes effective to plan several short visits at different times during the day or week.

The Internet

A growing number of schools and households have computer technology that allows access to the incredible amount of information available on the Internet.

ADVANTAGES

- The most obvious advantage of the Internet is the diversity and magnitude of information students can access – and the ease with which they can do so.

- The Internet and, in particular, the World Wide Web enable students to access sites it may be impossible to visit. Antarctic stations, NASA, and schools in other countries are just a few examples. This provides a wonderful breadth of information for the unit.

- The use of the Internet particularly suits the stage of investigation where individuals or small groups are following certain items of specific interest (see 'Going further'). Like surveys and interviews, information gathered may be down-loaded or printed and shared with the class.

- Electronic communication now means that students can seek information, on-line, from experts in the field. This technology adds a new dimension to letter writing, phone calls, faxes, surveys and interviews. It should be used in addition to these methods – not as a replacement for them.

- Students may also come across interactive projects through the Internet. For example, in finding out more about whales, they might discover other groups who are gathering information and recording data about whales. Students all over the world are currently using the Internet as a way to share data gathered with others and to contribute to a range of action programs.

- Internet use also develops research skills such as using key words, using ratings, making notes and selecting relevant information.

SOURCES

- Schools linked to the Internet will need to select from a range of software and search tools. Most education departments now have advisers in information technology, and more and more schools are employing teachers to work specifically in this role.

- Directories for the WWW (both in book and CD form) are available and updated each year. These can be a useful way to get started and to narrow down a search.

TEACHING POINTS

- Spend some time using search engines to explore the topic yourself. There may be particular sites that you wish to draw to students' attention – these can be reserved as 'bookmarks'.

- Make sure students know what they are looking for. A great deal of time can be wasted on fruitless Internet hunting.

- Small groups of students can work together at the computer. This encourages interaction and discussion as well as helping them learn technical skills from each other.

Students using computer technology to gather information.

3

STRATEGIES

for sorting out ...

BROAD PURPOSES

- to provide students with various means of processing and representing information and ideas arising from the finding-out stage
- to allow for a diverse range of outcomes
- to encourage students to begin to apply and transfer some of the information they have gained to a range of tasks or contexts
- to develop skills in the arts, mathematics, language and technology
- to assist students to explore some of the feelings, values and attitudes associated with the topic
- to create concrete records of experience and information gathered through the arts, mathematics, language and technology
- to encourage students to review what they know as a group

About this stage of a unit

The following strategies are used to help students make sense of the experiences they have had and the information they have gathered so far in the unit. As teachers, we sometimes make the assumption that the intended outcomes of an experience have been met. In reality, students will take very different things away from a shared experience. A trip to the zoo might be better remembered for the events during lunch time than the animals themselves. The sorting-out strategies are designed to help students revisit and work with the information they gathered and to share and compare it with others. By applying information gathered to, for example, a role-play, a model, a graph, a musical composition or a written report, students can experience purposeful and authentic use of drama, technology, maths, art and language respectively.

By working with the data through these different process areas, students' understandings of the topic deepens and broadens. For example, when the data gathered about animal habitats is explored through mathematics, visual art and music, the student revisits the information in different contexts and learns something new each time. Importantly, the activities in this section cater for the *differences* between students' learning styles – be they more auditory, visual or kinaesthetic learners, the integrated unit should offer opportunities for all to explore and express their understandings in a way that maximises their potential. This does not mean that students need to be working on different kinds of activities, rather that over the course of this stage, a *range* of suitable processes are used (Pigdon & Woolley 1992). The sorting-out stage not only caters for the range of learning styles or 'intelligences' (Gardner 1983) in the classroom, it also reflects the diversity of forms of perception and expression available to us as human beings.

> Outside of school, learners do not use only reading and writing to create and share meaning. They have multiple sign systems available, including music, art, maths, movement and drama … any of these sign systems can be vehicles for learning and teaching in a particular inquiry or for sharing that inquiry. (Short et al. 1996, p. 11)

It is at this stage of a unit where specialist teachers in the school often become more specifically involved. The music teacher, for example, may work with students to help them create a composition expressing what they have experienced or learned about the topic. The art teacher may help students design a visual art work based on the information they have gathered; a technology specialist might work with students to help them to design a multimedia stack or to use software for making graphs of their data.

The ways in which students can explore and communicate their understandings, feelings and values about a topic are limited only by their imagination (and the time and resources available). The strategies suggested in this chapter are open ended and encourage a range of outcomes. They can also be applied to many different topics. While the emphasis during the activity is on the content, students will be simultaneously be developing a wide range of *skills* across the key learning areas involved.

While the arts, mathematics, language and technology have been treated separately, strategies from each will often be combined. For example, a role-play (drama) might be recorded on video (media) and may use sounds to enhance its effectiveness (music). It may then be recorded as a script (language). The most important criteria in selecting these strategies is that the task 'suits' the information gathered and ultimately helps the students move closer towards an understanding of the topic.

Each key learning area offers its own particular way of organising ideas and information and therefore provides a unique perspective to the students' developing understandings. You are therefore encouraged to select sorting-out activities from several learning areas – provided they support your planned understandings.

Sorting out through dance and drama

Strategy	Description	Sample application
Free movement	Using background music or simple drum/tambour beats, students use their bodies to respond to an experience or represent observations.	Following a trip to the zoo, students show the relationship between structure and function by mimicking the movement of certain animals.
Freeze frame	In small groups, students create a 'human photo' to represent a scene or series of scenes. There is no sound or movement in the presentation.	This can be used to represent observations or understandings gained from a wide range of topics. For example, students may use freeze frame to show the way a rainforest is organised into layers; to show the before and after effects of natural disasters; or to show a common scene from family or neighborhood life.

Year 1 students use 'freeze frame' to represent a kangaroo with her joey.

Using mime to demonstrate understandings about cultural rituals.

Mime	Similar to freeze frame – but this activity allows for movement. Either individually or in small groups, students act out a short scene or event without sound.	A wide range of applications. This is a powerful way to recall observations made during a direct experience, such as an excursion. Very appropriate for topics that deal with aspects of human behavior and relationships.
The conscience game	The conscience game uses moral dilemmas to challenge students with contrasting values and issues that surround a particular topic. The teacher (or students themselves) designs a short scenario about the topic in which a difficult decision must be made. The issue is then analysed and argued using what students have	From a unit on healthy food: *You are at a party and have just had a big slice of delicious chocolate cake. You are still hungry and you notice that there are several slices left on the platter. There is also a plate of fruit on the table. What will you do?*

Strategy	Description	Sample application
	learned about the topic to support or challenge suggestions.

Organise students into teams of three. Student A presents arguments 'for' and student B presents arguments 'against'. They stand either side of student C – the final decision-maker.

Students A and B take it in turns to convince student C of their point of view. They argue in the first person – as the voice of student C's conscience.

Students could create their own dilemmas and present them to each other. | From a unit on caring for the local environment:
You are out with a new group of friends for the first time. You really want to be part of this group and you are having a great time. You each buy a hamburger for lunch and some of the kids throw their empty containers in the street You know they should put their rubbish in the bin but you are nervous about saying something to them. What will you do? |

Students engage in the 'conscience game'.

| **Puppet plays** | Using commercially made puppets or, preferably, puppets made by students, short plays are performed to demonstrate an aspect of the topic being explored.

Puppet types can include finger puppets; puppets made from gloves, old socks, paper bags; cardboard cut-outs attached to sticks; puppets sewn from fabric. Once made, puppets can also be used by students as a play activity where the topic is explored in a less structured way. | Some applications of this strategy include:
• re-creating parliament/local council after investigating processes and procedures in decision-making
• after a walk around the local community, showing people carrying out their various duties (shop keepers, police officers, etc) |
| **Role-play** | Role-play activities can be a powerful way for students to process the different beliefs, values and attitudes that people hold about a topic. It is also an excellent context for the development of skills in oral language, decision-making and group work. | Role-play activities are suitable for a wide range of topics – particularly those about which people have different beliefs. |

Strategy	Description	Sample application
	Provide students with a scenario relevant to your planned understanding and allocate appropriate roles. Scenarios can be selected from a real-life event (eg a conservation issue in the local community) or a book, or they can be created to suit the topic. Students discuss the issue in role with the aim of generating some solutions or recommendations. Students will bring to the role-play any information they have gained about the topic so far. It will also help them to consider their own views about the topic.	*Families*: Family members are faced with the decision about how best to care for an aging grandparent. They have different views about what is best. *Heritage*: A large entertainment centre is being proposed to replace a historic picture theatre. *Endangered animals*: A rare butterfly has been found on a site marked for a community housing development.

Role-play cards for a unit on water conservation.

Tourism / Finance
You are a big business man interested in attracting "money" to the town. You think the town will benefit from your decision.

Long-residing Mayor
You are ultimately responsible at the decision end! You have lived in the town for many years. You have ideas about change.

Council Member
The ratepayers have elected you to represent all of them fairly, eg farmers, unemployed, shop owners.

Environmental
You are concerned about the impact of the working of the factory on the environment.

Talk shows

The host of a talk show all about families.

Modelled on the television-style talk show, this activity allows students to express their understanding about a topic in a fun way. One child (or the teacher) acts as the host. Special guests are called on to be interviewed about an aspect of the topic. They may or may not be in role. Members of the audience (the rest of the class) ask questions.

The talk show may be videoed for later reference and to make the experience more authentic. Using a real or 'mock' microphone can also add to the fun.

This activity works well when students have been gathering information about different aspects of the topic. The talk-show set-up allows them to share with others what they have learned independently, for example:

- For a topic on 'space' students are interviewed as scientists with expertise about particular planets.
- For a topic on 'our neighborhood', students are interviewed about various services available in the local community.

Strategy	Description	Sample application
Simulations  *Props for children to use in a 'free-play' simulation of space travel.*	Simulations are a wonderful way to help students really 'get inside' a topic. In a simulation activity, aspects of the topic are 'lived out' as closely as possible to the real thing. Over a sustained period of time, students (often in role) mimic activities, events or experiences relevant to the topic. Use props to help create the scene.	Sample simulations for unit topics include: *Early settlers*: The classroom is set up to mimic life in the 1800s. *Trade*: Displays are created to represent various countries and their import/export products. Negotiations are then made between countries to buy and sell goods. *Shopping*: Areas of the room are set up to mimic certain kinds of shops, and students role-play the buying and selling process. *Leadership*: Students simulate a sitting of parliament.

Sorting out through media and visual arts

Strategy	Description	Sample application
Collage	Students paste various materials to paper or card to build up a visual image. Materials for collage can include: different paper types; magazine pictures; natural materials such as sand, old seeds, leaves (not living); newspapers; and fabrics.	Almost every unit topic lends itself to visual representation. Collage may be used to show the textures and contrasts in desert country, the contrasting materials and images of the city and country or the characteristics of different seasons.
Dioramas *A diorama for a unit of work on endangered species.*	Dioramas are 3D representations of a scene. One effective procedure is to use a box (eg shoe-box size) and place cut-out figures inside the box. Turn the box on its side and the bottom becomes a backdrop for the scene. Real items can also be used to bring the scene to life.	For a unit on marine life, dioramas can be used to show life in the depths of the ocean; for a unit on shelter, a diorama can become a 3D floor plan of a house.

Strategy	Description	Sample application
Models	Models give students an opportunity to represent what they are learning by re-creating experiences in a scaled-down way. Students can begin making models at the tuning-in stage of a unit and then add to or modify them throughout the investigation. Many materials are suitable for models, including construction materials, blocks, drinking straws, clay, plasticine, play dough, cardboard, wax, soft wire, fabric, boxes and other containers, and assorted 'junk' material. Models can be done on a small-scale, individual basis or may be large, group or even whole-class projects. For example, a model showing the layout of the local neighborhood.	Models are particularly useful for helping students to sort out ideas about the physical world. Models can be made, for example, of simple machines, water systems, insects, shelters, landforms, volcanoes, body systems, habitats, and so on.  *A 3D model of the local neighborhood.*
Visual artwork paint, crayon, charcoal, pencils, pastels, chalk	The experiences and information gathered at the finding-out stage of a unit may lend themselves to the use of particular media for visual representation. Provide students with the opportunity to choose from and work with various media to visually represent their ideas. Techniques such as using chalk on wet paper, marbling, combining water color and pastel, dot painting, and using different textured paper can all be introduced.	Visual representation is a form of processing and expression that will be appropriate for most topics. It can be used to represent an experience, a sequence of events, a feeling, or an idea. One way of using visual art at this stage of a unit is to ask students to consider the information they have gathered so far and to use the materials to show 'something you have discovered/learned/felt' about the topic so far.

Five-year-olds' representation of rainforest animals.

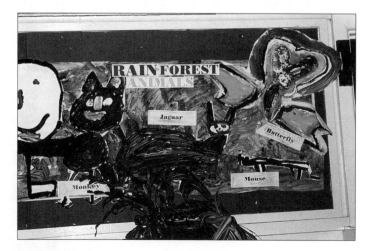

Strategy	Description	Sample application
Diagrams X-ray, comic strips, flow charts, cut-aways, maps, before-and-after	Students draw and label diagrams to demonstrate how something works, moves, behaves, etc. Various diagrammatic styles can be used, including 'X-ray' diagrams, sequential images, before-and-after illustrations, pictorial flow charts, symbols, cut-always and maps.	Many topics lend themselves particularly well to this form of graphic representation. For example, students could use diagrams to show how a tadpole grows and changes to a frog; how a particular transport system is organised; how a circuit works; or the stages in developing an advertising campaign.
Using fabrics quilts, patchwork, wall hangings, puppets, table cloths, dolls and other figures	Working with fabrics requires particular skills that are quite different from the challenges of paper and pencils. Using fabrics to create a response to experience can result in wonderful, enduring products that demonstrate what students have learned. Fabrics can be combined with fabric paint, buttons, sequins and beads. Some ideas for fabric use include: simple 'quilts' where each child designs and creates one square for a large patchwork; puppets (see above); wall hangings on which items are sewn, or painted; topic-based table cloths; felt dolls, animals and other figures.	The history of the local area can be represented as a patchwork 'story'; dolls can be made or dressed to show what students have learned about people in other cultures; the geography of an area can be represented on a fabric map. *A class mural representing a journey from Vietnam to Australia.* 
Making videos	The process of planning, filming, editing and viewing a video involves a wide range of skills and, in itself, is a valuable vehicle for learning. Footage from the finding-out stage (of interviews, guest	This activity is appropriate for most topics – depending on the nature of the data gathered. Students studying 'creatures in our backyards' might make a video explaining what and

Strategy	Description	Sample application
	speakers, excursions, etc) can be combined with commentaries from students explaining the significance of the information. Videos can take the form of roving reports or news style narrative and combine music and visual arts to enhance the effect.	where such creatures can be found; a topic exploring friendship or relationships might include interviews with groups of friends and short scenarios around the friendship theme; a unit looking at safety could present various scenarios showing how to respond to dangerous situations.
Multimedia presentations	As more schools have access to multimedia resources, students have some wonderful opportunities to analyse, record and communicate their findings to others. Students' use of multimedia to organise and present data will obviously depend on the equipment and software available in the school. Multimedia presentations can be worked on throughout the unit, as data is gathered, and presented in the final stage.	Students could design and present an investigation into their own family history using multimedia devices. A lot of software is available in the area of natural history. Students can combine this with their own research on animals and plants to develop presentations.
Mobiles	A mobile can be an effective way to present ideas and information. Mobiles can also allow students to show a particular sequence of events – or the way one thing is connected to another – by physically joining them. Simple mobiles can be made by drawing or writing on pieces of card and attaching these to lengths of string suspended from a common structure.	The life-cycle of a particular plant or animal can be represented in mobile form – each stage hanging from the one before. For a unit on energy, students could show the way the various sources of energy are connected to the Sun, using the Sun as the centre of the mobile. For a unit on space, a mobile could show the relative size of each planet.
Radio plays	Recording dialogue in the form of a play, interview, talk show or news broadcast focuses students on sound rather than vision as a form of communication. Students can prepare short radio plays and deliver them through the school's speaker system – sharing their unit investigations with others.	A unit on advertising or the media lends itself well to this form of sorting out. Students can write their own copy and jingles for advertisements. Combining music and other sound effects with a short explanation suits topics such as the sea or waterways; transport; other cultures; safety in the home; or natural disasters.

Strategy	Description	Sample application
Thaumatropes	Tie a length of string to either end of a piece of card. Twist the string at both ends and then pull so the card spins around. Images drawn on each side of the card will create an illusion as the card spins, looking as if they are part of the same scene. For example, a bird on one side and a nest on another will look like a bird in a nest when spun very fast.	Thaumatropes can be made for various topics that connect two concepts, for example: an animal or plant in its habitat.

Sorting out through mathematics

Strategy	Description	Sample application
Classifying	Classifiying and organising data – including objects, events and ideas – is an essential part of the sorting-out process. It is often the first step in organising information gained at the sorting-out phase of a unit. This classification can be a simple grouping of found objects, or a more complex organisation according to set criteria.	For example, young students investigating life in the marine environment may classify various sea creatures according to features, color or size. Older students might classify machines according to the energy form and source they use.
Fact finding	As students investigate a topic, they could be encouraged to record any mathematical facts they come across in books and other resources. These facts can then be translated into some kind of visual or other form to be explained to others.	For example, in a unit of work on structures, students could find out facts about the world's tallest building, widest bridge, oldest built structure, and so on.

Strategy	Description	Sample application
Graphs pictographs, pie graphs, line graphs, bar graphs, 3D graphs, dot graphs, stem plots	Graphing is one of the most common ways students can work with quantitative data gathered for a unit of work. Various graph forms should be explored. Computer databases are an excellent tool for recording and working with data in a unit and give students the opportunity to work with more complex graph forms.	Any unit in which students gather and record quantifiable data may lend itself to graphing information. Some examples include litter in the school ground; occupations of parents; family structures; physical data such as height, weight, eye and hair color; favorite pets; and foods. The important thing is that the graphing activity helps students to learn more about the topic.

A pictograph about families.

A maths project outline for year 6 students studying South-East Asia.

| **Maths projects** | Some units of work do not lend themselves as strongly to the integration of maths as others. Where a unit does not harness maths directly, teachers might choose to plan a complementary maths project that runs alongside the unit – working with some relevant information or ideas from the unit. Maths projects that involve students in a series of maths-based activities related to the topic are set for the class, small groups or individuals. This project may be worked on as a homework task during the course of a unit. | For example, an integrated unit on South-East Asia could be linked with a complementary maths project requiring students to find out about travelling distances to particular countries in Asia, flight times and exchange rates.

For a unit of work exploring transport, a complementary maths unit might require students to work through a sequence of activities on mapping, speed, distance and fuel consumption.

A unit of work for younger students on cooking and eating might involve a simple maths project on temperatures, weights and measures, volume and capacity, and so on. |

Strategy	Description	Sample application
Maps	Many topics involve students in exploring places in and around their local environment. Using published maps as part of that investigation, and recording findings on a map, are other ways that maths can be used to process and represent data. The extent to which the map is drawn to scale and includes conventional symbols and keys will depend on the level and experiences of students. Maps can be drawn up early in the unit and then added to at the end.	Any topic related to the concepts of place and space may lend itself well to maps and mapping. Maps can also be drawn up to record the journey to or layout of a site visited for finding out – for example, a map of the local park, the zoo, the school or the shopping centre. Cumulative maps will be developed as students find out more about the topic, for example a large map showing the location and features of the country's river system.

Eight-year-olds work cooperatively to prepare a map of an animal sanctuary.

Strategy	Description	Sample application
Problem-solving	Once students have gathered data about a topic, you can construct mathematical problems for them to solve, using the data they have gathered. The problem should be such that students apply or work with the data they have gathered so far in the unit. Once they have tackled a few problems, students can them create their own for others to solve. Encourage students to reflect on the mathematical processes they needed to apply to the problem-solving task.	In a unit of work on homes and habitats, students design a new enclosure to replace an outdated one at the zoo. The enclosure must fit existing space. In a unit of work on healthy eating, students must plan a healthy meal for a family within a given budget. In a unit of work on packaging, students design (and make) a reusable or recyclable package to fit a certain item.

Strategy	Description	Sample application
Scale models and drawings	As for models (see page 72), but there is an expectation that the model or drawing will be 'to scale'. This requires students to have measurement data about the original and to consider how the model is presented in terms of the proportions of various parts.	With younger students, this can be used simply to reinforce understandings about relative size. For example, a scale model of the life-cycle of a chicken should show correct relative sizes of egg to young chick, to older chicken, to hen/rooster. For older students, more specific measurement will be involved in, for example, a scale model of a building, an animal, or a machine.
Timelines	Timelines can be a very effective way of plotting data related to change or growth. Timelines can be combined with pictures or other forms of visual representation. They may be informal – simply using a before/after, then/now approach – or they might be more accurate representations showing intervals between times, days, dates, etc. Timelines can be drawn up by individual students or could be a whole-class project. A timeline can be created to run along the length of the room – or corridor – or around the school. Try making a hanging timeline as a mobile or creating a timeline as a patchwork wall-hanging with fabric.	For a unit of work on light, a timeline might show the way shadows change over the course of the day; in a unit of work on toys, a timeline might show the way one person's preference for different toys changed as they grew older. A unit of work on Aboriginal culture could include a timeline showing the sequence of events before and after European invasion. A unit of work on popular culture might include a timeline on fashion trends. A timeline is an effective way to demonstrate the relatively short time humans have been on the Earth compared with other life forms.
Venn diagrams	Venn diagrams help students to see patterns, similarities and differences among the data they gather. By placing actual objects, pictures or words in overlapping circles or other shapes, they are able to establish common and unique features within their data. Venn diagrams can be drawn or written, or they may be created using hoops and objects.	Venn diagrams can be used to explore the common and unique features of various animal and plant groups, types of rocks and crystals, forms of communication, roles of people in the community or in a family, and so on.

Sorting out through music

Strategy	Description	Sample application
Chants	Students use key statements or words gathered during the finding-out stage and create a chant to share with others. This can be accompanied by clapping, percussion instruments and simple actions. Existing chants familiar to students would be a good starting point. They substitute the words for language and information generated in the unit.	For example, students finding out about animal homes might create rhythmic chants based on their knowledge: Bandicoots in burrows Parrots in the trees Snakes inside a hollow log Dolphins in the seas
Raps	These are similar to chants. Students use the structure and beat of a rap to communicate what they have found out in their investigations. You may find it easiest to establish a rhythm first and agree to the form of the rap before students work with the language. Raps can them be performed for others in the school.	
Round the campfire	In the tradition of campfire stories, students create a descriptive text reflecting the experiences and/or information gained so far in the unit of work. The text can be written as a whole-class activity and recorded on a large chart. Sound effects, using body percussion, voices, instruments and so on, are then added to certain passages in the story. Students read the passage as a group and accompany it with sounds in marked places. The activity could also be done with descriptive passages taken from books read as part of the unit. Record the story to listen to at other times.	Any topic or text that lends itself to description can make use of this strategy. For example, young students finding out about various animals might jointly construct a simple description of those they have seen at the zoo. As it is read out, sound effects are used for animal sounds, movement, habitat. For technology-based units, descriptions of machines could be accompanied by sound effects, and even a walk around the neighborhood can become a 'round the campfire' experience on retelling.

Strategy	Description	Sample application
Soundscapes	This strategy is best used in conjunction with visual arts or drama presentations. Students use recorded music or their own composition to select appropriate 'background' sound for particular scenes or images.	For example, students who have been investigating the topic 'Life in the desert' could find pieces of music that express what they have learned about the landscape, the animals, the plants and the general conditions. Young students exploring the properties of water can compose 'music' to represent rain, ice and steam. Musical accompaniments can be devised for a unit of work looking at insects: what piece would we choose for a butterfly? a bee? a preying mantis? If multimedia technology is available in the school, sound can be recorded together with images in a computerised 'slide show' production.
Composition	Many topics will involve students in exploring feelings and emotions as they gather data and gain new experiences. Music can be a wonderful vehicle for them to express those feelings – either their own or others'. Students should be encouraged to create their own music in response to experiences they had at the finding-out stage. If a video, film, play or novel has been used to provide students with information or ideas about the topic, they could compose or explore sounds to represent the feelings of various characters.	For example, in a unit of work on 'growing older' students might have visited a home for the elderly to interview older people about their lives. Ask them to find or create a piece of music that explains how they felt in that environment. Excursions into the outdoors for environmental units can prompt some wonderful musical responses.
Musical stories	Music can be used to tell a story. Encourage students to either compose their own music or seek out recorded sounds that they can bring together to tell a story based on what they have learned in the unit so far. This strategy works best with something sequential.	Students can use music to tell the story of the way a caterpillar becomes a butterfly; the way a house is built; the journey of a food item from the land to our table, and so on.

Sorting out through English

Many of these strategies can be used with languages other than English, depending on the students' level of competence and experience.

Strategy	Description	Sample application
Writing using a range of text types Personal descriptions Technical descriptions Scientific reports Explanations Instructions Manuals Recipes Directions Reviews Diaries Personal recounts Stories Fables Fairy tales Poems Letters Advertisements Charts Scripts Banners	Different units of work lend themselves to different forms of texts and, therefore, to different forms of writing. When sorting out the information they have gathered, students can be encouraged to explore various ways of constructing texts for different purposes. These purposes can include: • to describe • to explain • to persuade • to argue • to instruct • to narrate/ tell a story • to reflect • to report The nature of the content with which students are working will partly determine the genre – or combination of genres – that they choose to work with but, more importantly, the actual information they gather and the purpose for which they write will be the main guide. (See Wing Jan 1991; Derewianka 1990; Green 1992)	In a unit of work on the gold rush, students visit a simulated gold-mining town. They then write narrative recount texts – composing stories about life on the goldfields. In a unit on advertising, students create their own mock advertisements for various products. To do this they use persuasive and descriptive text. In a unit on water, students find out about the journey of water from the river to the sea. They record this information in the form of an explanation. In a unit on keeping healthy, students find out how important it is to exercise and eat a balanced diet. They write a piece arguing for more time for exercise in the school day. In a unit exploring reptiles, students find out about the various classifications within this animal group. They write a report outlining the features of each sub-group. In a unit on inventions, students write a set of instructions to tell others how to operate a particular device.

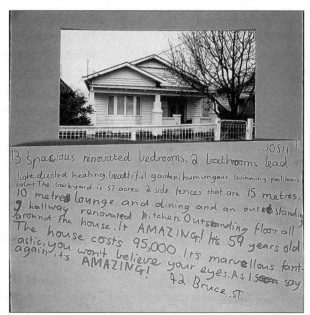

Using persuasive language in a unit of work on housing.

Strategy	Description	Sample application
Build a story	This strategy can be an effective way to record an experience or create a response to one. A student or the teacher provides the beginning of the story and writes it on a large piece of paper. The paper is then passed from student to student or group to group and they add a section to it in a given time period. The story or recount is then shared with the class and modified for improvement.	The strategy works particularly well following a whole-class shared experience. For example, after a visit to a farm, young students take it in turns to contribute a sentence to a recount of their experiences.
Compare and contrast	This is a useful way to help students analyse the information gained from two or more information sources. Draw up a chart of two columns with the headings of each source (eg two guest speakers) at the top. Record summary statements about issues arising from the first source. Use the second column to compare the way the issue or topic was dealt with in the second source.	This strategy is useful within units that generate different views, values and feelings. For example, a compare-and-contrast chart could be made to show the way two elderly people viewed their childhood in the local neighborhood. Information about different elements of the same topic can be compared in this way. For example, in a unit on invertebrates, a snail and a spider could be compared and contrasted in relation to their defence mechanisms.
Data charts  *A data chart for a unit of work on farms.*	This is similar to a compare-and-contrast chart but can work with more information across a greater variety of sources. Data charts are a very effective, concrete way of sorting information and helping students see patterns emerging across data. Data charts can be constructed individually, in small groups or as a whole-class display. They are set up in grid form, with categories determined for each row and each column. Headings for rows and columns take the form of questions, topics or information sources. Students build up the data chart over the course of the unit. One effective technique is to write on colored squares of paper and	Ideas and information can be recorded on a data chart of almost every topic. Some examples include: • For the unit of work on reptiles – different species are listed across the data chart and questions related to appearance and behaviors are written down the side. Information is then recorded for each species. • For a unit of work called 'Discovering Australia', significant events in history are written across the top of the data chart and sources of information are written down the side. Summaries of the way each source describes the event are provided in the boxes.

Strategy	Description	Sample application

then pin or paste these to a large roll of paper. The use of colors enables the information to be analysed quickly.

Many computer software programs allow students to enter data on a spreadsheet in a similar way. This can then be 'sorted' using a variety of criteria. It could also be the basis for visual representation, graphs or factual texts.

Data charts can also be used to record raw data gathered from interviews, experiments and observations.

Five-and six-year-olds combine English, maths and art in a data chart about pets.

ANIMAL	FOOD	COLOUR	HABITAT	SIZE	MOVEMENT	LEGS
CHICKEN		rad and bai		l l		2
QUAIL		Yellow		l l		2
GUINEA PIGS		bain		l l		4
MALTESE TERRIER		Whitet		l l	ran	4
RABBIT		black		l l	hop	2
CAT	baith	grey		l l		4
BUDGIE		Yellow		l l		2
DOGS		brown		l l		4

DRTA

Directed reading and thinking activities can be used together with the texts provided to help students gather information about the topic.

Basically, this procedure involves either the teacher or students reading the text up until a given point. Students then discuss their ideas and make predictions about what might follow. More of the text is read and further predictions made at another point. The activity works well when students have some understandings about the topic to bring to the text. In this way they can make an informed prediction.

The use of this strategy is dependent on the kinds of texts you are using in the unit of work. Narrative or information narrative texts lend themselves well to the strategy.

Strategy	Description	Sample application
Oral presentations	Individual, paired or small-group oral presentations can be used as a way to respond to an experience and share information gathered about a topic. Oral reports should have a clear structure and purpose, with a view to informing the audience. Oral reports should be kept short and may be accompanied by work done, say, in the visual arts area. Students need time to 'rehearse' their report and, therefore, may benefit by repeating the report to several small groups. Use video or tape recorders to keep a record of the reports for self- and teacher-assessment purposes. *As part of a unit on Asia, year 6 students present information about Indonesia to the class.*	Oral reports work most effectively when students are sharing information that hasn't been gathered by the whole class. For example, students visiting the zoo may each have had a different animal to focus on. Their oral reports then provide others with information about the animal they studied. 
Told us ... made us wonder	This is a simple structure for a retrieval chart following a shared experience. Draw up two columns on a large sheet of paper. At the top of the chart, write the name of the experience, book, guest speaker or venue. Label two columns with the phrases 'told us ...' and 'made us wonder ...' Students then suggest ideas for each column. The 'told us' column summarises the information gained from the experience and the 'made us wonder' includes any questions, issues, problems or areas of confusion arising from the experience. *A chart compiled after sharing the big book **Somewhere in the Universe**.*	This strategy can follow any finding-out experience. For example, in a unit of work on disabilities, a guest speaker might come in to talk to students about the challenges of living with a disability. This will, no doubt, raise many questions and issues for students which can be recorded along with information gained, on the chart. 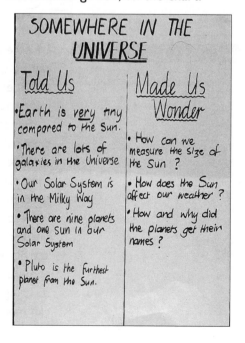

Caption for the Told Us / Made Us Wonder chart:

SOMEWHERE IN THE UNIVERSE

Told Us
- Earth is very tiny compared to the Sun.
- There are lots of galaxies in the Universe
- Our Solar System is in the Milky Way
- There are nine planets and one Sun in our Solar System
- Pluto is the furthest planet from the Sun.

Made Us Wonder
- How can we measure the size of the Sun?
- How does the Sun affect our weather?
- How and why did the planets get their names?

Strategy	Description	Sample application

Written conversation	This strategy is just as it sounds – students talk to each other in writing. It works very well as a follow-up to a shared experience but should not be a long-winded, laborious activity. Written conversations usually take an 'interview' form with one student asking the other about their opinions and responses to the experience. One fun way to do this is to give each pair one piece of paper and a time limit. The task is for student A to find out as much as they can about student B's views within the given time.
	
	    An adaptation of this task is to ask students to write to each other in role – based on key characters emerging in the unit. Written conversations can be used as the basis for writing the script for a play or a puppet performance.
		Following a visit to the market for a unit of work on food, students may 'talk to each other on paper' about their favorite part of the excursion, what they liked and didn't like, and so on. Then they report back to the whole class.
		
		    Students studying family life might work through a written conversation between a parent and child about a particular issue or problem.
		
		    Characters from books could form the basis for the roles students take in this activity. For example, in a unit of work on marine life, the story *Storm Boy* might be read. Students then construct written conversations between Mr Percival and Storm Boy.

Wall stories and charts	This activity is a popular way of recording experiences. As well as providing an opportunity to recall and process the information gained, a wall story or chart can then be the basis for many language activities – word study, bookmaking, and so on.
	
	    Most wall stories are recounts of experiences or observations. The type of text you use will depend on the topic and the purpose. Discuss this with students beforehand. These texts can be constructed as a whole-class activity, but this often means that a few students dominate while others lose interest as the teacher scribes. This can be overcome by having small groups working with the teacher while others are working independently. The whole class can then come together to read and revise the text.
	
	    Using an overhead projector, or projecting a computer screen onto the wall, can offer more efficient ways of recording language.
		Wall stories or charts are wonderful ways to record procedural events that took place on an excursion. For example, in a unit of work on the origins of food, students might visit a bakery where they see the process of bread-baking. This process is then retold in writing after the event.
		
		    Students growing seeds might gradually develop a shared, procedural text outlining the stages the plant went through and the things that needed to be done to nurture it.

Strategy	Description	Sample application
Read and retell	The read and retell technique can be a useful way to help individual students make sense of the texts being used in the unit. Essentially, this technique requires the students to retell in their own words something they have read. They are usually asked to focus on the main points of the story or report rather than the detail. Read and retell might only be carried out with students requiring more support in reading or it could be done in pairs as a whole-class activity.	The approach to read and retell used will depend on the text. If the text is a narrative, the focus for the retelling will be characters, setting, plots and main theme. If the text is factual, the focus would be on summarising the main points.
Three-level guide	This strategy enables students to read a text at different levels and to uncover the layers of meaning within the text. Use a text (oral, written or visual) that deals with an issue related to the unit of work being studied. Design statements about the text based on three levels of understanding: literal, interpretive and analytical. Students must indicate 'true' or 'false' in response • Students work through the task individually then share in groups. • Responses to the second and third groups of statements might involve students in lengthy discussions which could involve returning to the text to substantiate their viewpoint.	For example – to help analyse a text about insects: 1. Literal – statements related directly to the text: *Insects are invertebrates* 2. Interpretive – statements that require the student to interpret information: *Insects have an important role to play in the food chain.* 3. Analytical – statements that require students to look at the 'big picture' – the broader issues in relation to the text: *Pesticides should not be used under any circumstances.*
Poetry	Using the language generated by the activities and experiences in the unit so far, students can be encouraged to write poetry that expresses understandings and/or feelings about what has been learned. Standard forms of poetry (haiku, limerick, rhyming prose, etc) can be used, or students could explore their own form. The nature of the topic and information gained should be considered when	Writing poems will suit many topics, particularly those that lend themselves to rich description or reflection, or to the expression of feelings.

Strategy	Description	Sample application
	selecting the style of poetry to be used. If appropriate, share other poems written about the topic – if they support the understandings around which the unit is planned. This will help to provide models for students' own writing.	
Bookmaking	Depending on the nature of the writing students do during the unit, some pieces may lend themselves to publication in book form. The creation of a book can be an ongoing task – beginning at the sorting-out stage and continuing on through to 'action' which could take the form of a book launch.	See 'Writing' using a range of text types (page 81).
Puzzle cards I have 6 legs I can fly I have spots What am I?	This may take the form of a 'Who/what am I?' puzzle. On one side of the card, students write down three clues to help the reader work out what is drawn or written on the other side of the card. The cards can be hung or placed around the room, or compiled to make a puzzle book.	Puzzle cards can be made for many topics – to describe animals, plants, famous people, occupations, places, special events, items of technology, and so on.
Readers theatre	This literacy strategy can be used in conjunction with novels or picture story books that have been read to support the unit content. In brief, simple scripts are written based on the book. Students take on various characters from the book and read their part of the script as appropriate. It is important that the book chosen for this activity links to the understandings planned – not just the unit topic.	For example, Shell Silverstein's book *The Giving Tree* could be scripted for readers theatre during a unit about conservation and the environment.

Sorting out through technology

For primary students in particular, the key learning area of technology is the basis for both the *content* of some units (for example, topics such as communication, toys, machines, past and present) and the *process* in which students engage across units. The basic process of technology mirrors the learning sequence through which students move during an inquiry-based unit. Just as students tune in, find out, sort out, make conclusions and reflect, so too do they investigate, design, produce and evaluate in technology.

An integrated unit of work is, therefore, an excellent context in which to learn about and through technology. There are many, many ways in which technology-based strategies can be used. Many of these are incorporated in the strategies already outlined. For example, using information technology in the finding-out stage; gathering and recording data in mathematics and selecting and using a range of materials to create products in the arts. While all these activities incorporate technology, it is important that the technology skills and processes are made explicit to students.

There are some topics which lend themselves particularly well to students working with technology in order sort out and present their learning to others. Some examples include:

Homes and habitats – students design, produce and evaluate a form of shelter

Transport – students design, produce and evaluate various forms of transport to suit certain criteria or conditions

Packaging – students investigate different forms of packaging then design, produce and evaluate a form for a particular purpose

Celebrations – students design, produce and evaluate an appropriate card to send to someone as part of a particular celebration

Water – students create a model to show the way water travels from the mountains to the sea

Energy – students investigate renewable forms of energy and create models of environmentally friendly housing or transport

For further guidance on the role of technology in curriculum, see T. Downes, & C. Fatoures, *Learning in an Electronic World*, PETA, Newtown, NSW 1995.

Students design and build models of houses, representing dwellings in different parts of Asia.

4 STRATEGIES

for going further

BROAD PURPOSES

- to extend and challenge students' understandings about the topic
- to provide more information in order to broaden the range of understandings held by students
- to meet the particular interests that have emerged during the unit
- to revise, where necessary, some of the key understandings relevant to the topic
- to develop independent research skills

About this stage of a unit

By this stage of a unit, students will be demonstrating new understandings and, perhaps, continued misconceptions about the topic. The strategies used at this point can be used to address these misconceptions and to extend understandings. While the title 'going further' suggests the gathering of more information, this may not be the case for all students. For some, this will be an opportunity to return to texts or experiences which they have not sufficiently understood.

Going-further tasks may also challenge or provide a *contrast* to the information gathered during the unit so far. The suggested strategies are particularly useful for addressing students' individual needs – allowing individual and small groups of students to follow personal pathways of interest or need.

The organisation of the class at this time might take the following forms:

- another whole-class, shared experience (such as those suggested in Chapter 2)

- small-group investigations into specific aspects of the topic

- individual or shared projects or contracts

- a combination of independent activity for some students and small group or individual revision work with others

Many teachers choose not to plan the activities for this stage of the unit until students are well into the investigation. The stage can be skipped altogether – or can be designed to meet interests and needs as they emerge. Indeed, individual or team contracts and projects can be used throughout the unit, running parallel to the whole-class investigation.

Individual projects

When projects are introduced to students in the context of a whole-class investigation, they are more likely to understand the significance and see purpose in the task.

BASIC PROCEDURE

- Begin by revisiting any questions or issues that have emerged through the unit so far. Identify any aspects that students still want to find out more about.

- Return to your planned understandings and consider those that need stronger emphasis.

- Brainstorm possible topics within the broader unit topic that could be explored through projects. For example: a unit on transport might give rise to projects about individual forms of transport; a unit on animals might include projects on particular species; a unit on life-cycles might look at the way different cultures care for the elderly, and so on.

- Allocate topics to individuals, pairs or trios.

- Students then brainstorm a list of key questions they wish to find out about.

- The most important thing is for each child or group to have a clear set of questions to guide their project work. There may be some common questions that all students address within the scope of their project.

- Discuss the various ways that projects might be presented. The traditional sheet of colored card is one presentation possibility. See 'Sorting out' for others.

- Establish a clear timeline in which projects must be completed.

MODIFICATIONS

- This could be given to older students as a homework task through the latter part of the unit.

TEACHING POINTS

- Projects, particularly those carried out for homework, often suffer from plagiarism. Remind students of the importance of presenting the information they gather in their own words.

- If the projects are to be displayed, they should be treated as 'published' texts and, therefore, will require drafting, conferencing and editing.

- Allocate regular times during the week/s to view and discuss work in progress.

Contracts

These are similar to projects; however, they often require greater independence and are usually carried out by individuals.

BASIC PROCEDURE

- A contract can be drawn up as a series of tasks – negotiated between student and teacher – that must be completed by a given date.

- You could design a similar framework for all students to follow, with opportunities for each student to include tasks they wish to carry out in relation to their own interest.

- The contract should be written up, a deadline for completion negotiated, and the contract signed by teacher and students.

- Contracts may be a useful structure for homework tasks during the unit.

MODIFICATIONS

- The content, layout and purpose of a contract will depend entirely on the topic and the needs of the students at this time in the unit.

- Once students are more familiar with the way a contract works, they will be able to suggest and negotiate tasks more realistically.

TEACHING POINTS

- Make sure that regular spot checks are made – especially when contracts are being completed as homework tasks.

- Some students will have less support from home and will require teacher guidance to meet their deadlines

---

Learning contract for unit of work:
'It's a small world'

- Choose one insect you would like to find out more about

Chosen insect for contract focus: _____bees_____

- We agree to complete the following tasks by (date) ___12·9·97___

- Gather and record information from at least 3 different sources about: :

life cycles   bee keeping   types of bees

- Make a model of our chosen insect

- Prepare a simple 'slide show' about what we have learned about our insect

- Give a short talk to the class about what we have learned

Students' signature *Ben and Sam*   Teachers' signature *Kath Murdoch*

An example of a learning contract for a unit of work.

Cooperative group tasks

By assigning specific tasks to small groups of students, you can meet the needs and interests of individuals while building the collective knowledge of the class. Activities for cooperative group work at this stage in the unit might be designed to gather more information or to apply the information already gathered.

BASIC PROCEDURE

- Organise students into small groups. These could be based on common interest or common needs. You could allow students to self-select if appropriate.

- Explain that each group has a task to help them gain more understanding about the topic.

- Design tasks that can be worked on by all students within the group. The emphasis is on working towards a shared goal. Tasks can be written on task cards and could include:
        simple experiments
        reading and responding to text
        discussion and decision-making
        making art works
        directed observations and record-keeping

- Each group must allocate roles to individuals to ensure that everyone in the group is involved in the task.

- Products are then shared with the whole group.

MODIFICATIONS

- You might choose to supply a common problem, issue or topic which each group then works on in their own way. Groups choose the form of response or product they will create during the session, for example:

    We have been investigating the experience of elderly people in various cultures. In your group, decide on one way we could improve the way we manage care of older people in our society.

    We have been investigating energy. Your group task is to design a classroom that will be more energy efficient.

    We have been learning all about pets and what we need to do to care for them. As a group, make/design/discuss/draw your ideal pet.

TEACHING POINTS

- When organising the groups, consider the needs of individuals within them and allocate tasks that will challenge or support students where necessary.

- Choose activities to which all students can bring some information gathered from the unit – the more open ended the activity the better.

- Revise the roles and responsibilities students can take within the group (time keeper, leader, gofer, etc).

- Reflect on the group processes during and after the activity:
    What did you do to ensure that your group worked well?
    What got in the way of the group working effectively?
    How could this be dealt with next time?

Expert groups

This popular grouping strategy (also called jigsaw grouping) encourages individuals to 'teach' others about what have they have learned. It can also be a useful way of working with a large body of information.

BASIC PROCEDURE

- Organise students into small home groups. These groups discuss the topic or task at hand and delegate each member to explore an aspect of the task. For example, the topic might be 'families' and each member is given a different aspect of family life to investigate, read about or gather information about (sources of conflict, composition, celebrations etc).

- Each member now moves into expert groups who share the same focus for investigation.

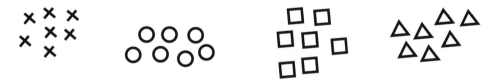

- Expert groups then dissolve and members return to their home groups to 'teach' to others the information they have gathered.

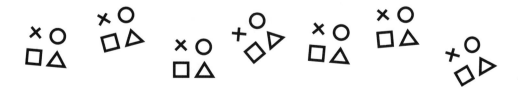

MODIFICATIONS

- This strategy can be used to deal with information in the space of one or two sessions or may be used to organise an investigation over a longer period of time.

TEACHING POINTS

- Students need to be reminded that they will be responsible for teaching others back in their home group. Older students should be encouraged to take notes to help them report back.

- A set of key questions for each expert group can facilitate the process.

- Young students can be given badges, headbands or some other form of identification to help them form the expert group.

Seven at once: multiple intelligence work stations

Using Howard Gardener's multiple intelligences as a framework, activities are designed to help the students extend their understanding of the topic in different ways. 'Seven at once' involves a significant amount of organisation, but is worth the result.

BASIC PROCEDURE

- Set up seven work stations around which groups of students will rotate during a session/day/week.

- Each station requires students to explore the topic through a different medium or 'intelligence'.

- In simple terms, these ways of knowing involve students in:
  - visual activities (drawing, painting, designing symbols, making models, etc)
  - mathematical activities (working with numbers, patterns, inductive and deductive thinking)
  - linguistic activities (writing, reading, oral language activities)
  - kinesthetic activities (movement, performance activities)
  - musical activities (using music, sound, rhythm to express ideas, listening to music)
  - interpersonal activities (communicating with others, decision-making and problem-solving in a group, etc)
  - intrapersonal activities (reflecting; feeling; forming beliefs, values, philosophies)

- Students move through each station either individually or as part of a team.

- Once all students have experienced each station, make a list of new ideas and understandings that have emerged.

MODIFICATIONS

- The seven ways of knowing can be used as the basis for activity in individual contracts.

- Choose only the areas that seem to lend themselves best to the topic.

- Activities may be quite structured and specific, or students can be encouraged to explore the topic in the given domain but to decide their own focus or product.

TEACHING POINTS

- One of the traps with using this approach is that activities can be undertaken in a more thematic style, without real consideration of what students are learning. It is important that the activities set up at each station support the planned understandings for the unit.

One example of the 7-at-once strategy in use, for the topic of inventions:

1. Verbal — linguistic

Choose a famous inventor we have learned about during the unit. Write a list of questions you would like to ask them if you met them today.

2. Visual — spatial

Think about an invention you would like to create. What is something that would make the world a better place? How would it work? Draw or make a model of the invention to show how it works.

3. Musical — rhythmic

Add to our tape of sounds that famous inventions make (eg telephone, computer, toothbrush). You may need to mimic the sounds by using your voice or instruments. Later, we will see if we can guess the invention by listening to your part of the tape.

4. Logical — mathematical

Think over some of the inventions we have discussed. See if you can plot them on a timeline. Now add possible inventions to the timeline that may be created in the future.

5. Bodily — kinesthetic

There are various old appliances and inventions on this table. Use the tools available to take them apart and see if you can work out how they actually work.

6. Interpersonal

Either:

explain how one of the inventions from station #5 works to someone else

or

role-play an interview with a famous inventor using the questions you wrote at station 1.

7. Intrapersonal

Reflect on these questions in your learning log:

What do you think is the invention that is most important in your life? Why?

Are there any inventions that you think have been bad for the world? Why?

Other independent activities for going further

Reading corners, where texts are read and responded to individually or in groups

Listening posts: one or more students listen to a tape through headphones

Viewing videos or pictures: (may also be revisiting videos seen earlier in the unit)

Activity sheets: designed to support understandings

Making models or other visual arts works

STRATEGIES

for making conclusions

BROAD PURPOSES

- to assist students to make conclusions and generalisations about the topic
- to assess and demonstrate students' progress towards the planned understandings, skills and values throughout the unit
- to inform further planning
- to encourage students to reflect on their learning
- to foster each student's ability to synthesise their learning and to see the 'big picture' ideas behind a topic
- to help students explore and justify their feelings and values related to a topic
- to provide a point of comparison for students between the ideas generated at the beginning of the unit and those evident now
- to develop metacognitive abilities

About this stage of a unit

In integrated curriculum, the emphasis in all our teaching is on helping students to make connections. This purpose, however, becomes most explicit at this stage of a unit.

As students move through an investigation, their prior knowledge is built upon and misconceptions are challenged and modified. The 'making conclusions' stage of a unit helps teachers and learners to evaluate the extent to which this had taken place. Deep understanding takes time, and achieving it is a gradual process that evolves throughout the unit (Gardner 1997). The depth of understanding gained by students will have been revealed in many of the activities so far, but these making-conclusions tasks are designed to refocus on the 'big ideas' that have underpinned the unit from the outset.

The following activities require students to think beyond the data they gathered and sorted in previous stages and to consider what they now *understand*. This is a time for big picture thinking – for stepping back from the investigation and asking:

What have I learned?
How do I feel about what I have learned?
How have my ideas changed?
Why have my ideas changed.
Where do I go from here?

The focus in these strategies often shifts back to a 'personalising' of the topic for individual students. As they consider how their understandings have evolved, the 'personal relevance' of the inquiry is evoked. Strategies help students to establish connections and identify patterns and relationships. Together with strategies for taking action, these tasks often encourage students to 'actively try out their mental maps in their own world' (Atkin 1993). Some of the strategies encourage students to explicitly transfer their knowledge or skills to a new context. Without 'transfer', knowledge remains inert, passive:

> To extend learning, to bridge the old to the new and to lead students toward relevant transfer across academic content and into life situations is, then, the mission of the thinking classroom. (Fogarty et al. 1991, p. xiii)

While assessment in an integrated program is 'built-in' and ongoing, the activities suggested in the following pages are particularly useful as focused assessment tasks. This stage is about drawing the threads together and comparing the learning achieved at this point in the investigation to that which was evident at the beginning. These activities assume that some understanding about the topic has been gained, and they help you and your students analyse just how strong this understanding is.

Importantly, the strategies suggested provide you with a window on aspects still needing attention – either at the whole-class, small-group or individual level. By analysing the student responses to the activities presented, you will have a clearer picture of what still needs to be developed, revisited, revised or challenged.

Products of several of these strategies can be shared with parents and others as a way of demonstrating the learning that has taken place in the unit. This should be a time of insight and celebration.

Board games

Making board games can be an excellent way for students to bring together the knowledge they have gained during a unit of work and to pass it on to others. This is also a very useful 'performance' based assessment task.

BASIC PROCEDURE

• Explain to the students that they are going to use the topic you have been studying as the basis of a board game – perhaps a game to teach other people something about the topic.

- Discuss the common features of board games. For example, dice are often used to determine how far you move around the board, players are competing to reach a destination, the board is organised into pathways along which you move a counter, and certain points are reached as you move along the pathway that can help or hinder your progress.

- These features are then adapted to the topic you have been exploring. For example, a board game based around the topic of endangered animals may include:

   - a destination of a national park where the animals are protected

   - a pile of cards from which children select when they land on a certain square. These cards may help or hinder progress.

MODIFICATIONS

- Students' use of this strategy will only be limited by their knowledge of how a board game works. Bring examples in to show them if necessary.

- If you think students might find the development of a board game difficult, provide the overall structure and format for them. Their job is to design the content of the game.

- The activity can be combined with art and technology – as students design and make the various components of the game, and even a box to store it in.

TEACHING POINTS

- This activity takes time and planning. It is more effective as a cooperative exercise where different students in a group take responsibility for different aspects of the game.

- Although it is presented as a making-conclusions activity, the final result can be used as a form of action as students present the game to others to play and learn.

Bloom's box

Bloom's taxonomy for thinking is used here as a structure to encourage students to think in different ways about what they have learned.

BASIC PROCEDURE

- Make a large dice using card. On each face of the dice, write questions using the framework provided:
  Knowledge: (eg: *What is one thing you have learned about forests?*)
  Comprehension (eg: *How do some animals use their forests for protection?*)
  Application (eg: *What other sorts of habitats do you know?*)
  Analysis (eg: *What are some of the things that can threaten the forest as a habitat for animals?*)

Synthesis (eg: *How can we help protect forests?*)

Evaluation (eg: *How do you feel about the logging of native forests?*)

- The dice is then 'rolled' by individual students who must provide an answer to the question facing up when it lands. The questions should be open ended, to allow for a range of responses.

MODIFICATIONS

- Once students are familiar with the taxonomy, they can construct their own questions.

- The activity can be adapted for younger students by using simpler questions, sentence beginnings or key words.

TEACHING POINTS

- This activity can be a useful way of setting the scene for making generalisations about the topic.

Concept maps

Concept maps are a valuable tool through which students can organise the ideas they have about a particular concept or topic. The essential feature of a concept map (in contrast to a flowchart or brainstorm) is the connections explicitly made between the key items on the map. For this reason, concept mapping is often easier for students to do at the end of a unit.

BASIC PROCEDURE

If introducing students to concept mapping, the following steps can be carried out using a very familiar topic. The procedure is then repeated for the unit topic.

- Give each student about 10 small cards.

- On one card, they write the word or phrase that is the subject for the concept map (eg *families*)

- On the remaining cards, they write or draw other words that they consider to be important about the topic.

- On big sheets of paper, students arrange the cards in a way that makes sense to them.

- Students must then show the way the ideas relate to each other. Lines or arrows are drawn between the related ideas. Words or connecting phrases are written on the line or arrow to make the connection clearer. (Brainstorming a list of possible connecting phrases is helpful here; these could include: *can be, produces, needs, relies on, affects, helps, is part of, is more important than*, and so on).

- Cards can be attached with removable adhesive to make reorganisation easier.

- Ask students to share maps and see if they can 'read' others.

- Generalisations can then be written on the basis of these concept maps.

MODIFICATIONS

- Pictures rather than words can be used, particularly with young children.

- You may wish to have students create a concept map from a predetermined set of words about the topic. Keep in mind, however, that the words students come up with are, in themselves, useful assessment data.

- Once students are familiar with the procedure, it is not necessary to use cards. They will become more adept at constructing their concept map directly on paper.

- Computer software that enables to user to link text with arrows can be a very useful tool for concept mapping, allowing students to experiment with different forms and arrangements before printing.

TEACHING POINTS

- Concept maps are often best done on an individual basis as they reflect the students' personal views of the topic.

- Generalisations can be formed on the basis of the connecting ideas shown on the map.

- Ask students to 'read' sections of their map to you. They should be able to read sensible phrases or even sentences within their map.

- Give students opportunities to revisit their maps at a later stage.

Connectit

This activity is rather like a human concept map. Using wool or string, students show connections between the key ideas within a topic. (Adapted from Pike & Selby 1998)

BASIC PROCEDURE

- Organise students into pairs or trios.

- Groups are located around the room – preferably in a circle.

- Give each group a ball of wool (a different color for each), a large sheet of paper and a marker pen.

- Each group is given one aspect of the topic that has been studied. For example, the topic of 'Keeping healthy' could include the following key aspects: fitness, diet, drugs, work and rest.

- Each group then brainstorms, on a large piece of paper, everything they know about that aspect of the topic.

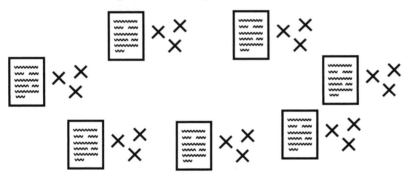

- Once the brainstorms are complete, one person in each group remains at that station. They hold the ball of wool.

- The other group members move around the room, reading and discussing the results of the various brainstorms and looking for ways in which the ideas within each are connected or linked.

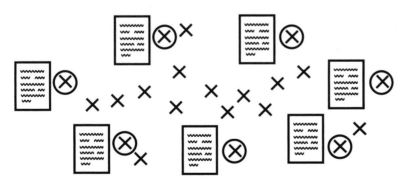

- Once a link has been discovered between two key ideas, the ball of wool is passed between those two 'stationary' group members. There must be agreement from both groups that the ideas are linked.

- Connections can be made between any groups – there is no limit to the number of links made. As more connections are made, it becomes less easy to move among the web of wool.

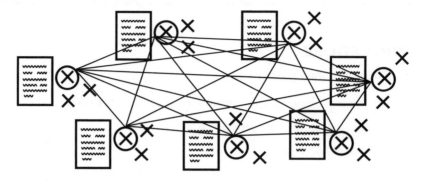

- The teacher decides when the activity should be stopped. Sometimes it comes to a natural conclusion when all the connections are made.

- Stop the activity and ask students to examine the connections they see between the various components of the topic. Individual groups can be asked to explain the connections they found. As they do so, their ball of wool can be wound up, gradually undoing the web.

MODIFICATIONS

- This activity can also be a useful way to show students the connections between topics. Each group is given one unit topic that has been explored in the year so far.

- Students can follow the activity by drawing their own web of connections

- The activity may also be used to explore the connections within one aspect of the topic. For example, if the topic was 'invertebrates', the activity could be used to show the food web of which they are a part.

TEACHING POINTS

- While the activity can be done with the whole class, space and patience is needed. It is more effective with between 12 and 20 students.

- Make sure students discuss the links they are going to make with each other. There must be agreement that the two ideas really do have a connection.

- Use the activity to explore the idea that, in life, everything is connected to everything else.

Content-based cloze

The cloze procedure is widely used to support students in learning to read. When the emphasis is on the content or meaning of a text, it can also be used as a useful assessment device for integrated units.

BASIC PROCEDURE

- Choose a text that has been used during the course of the unit (eg a factual big book) or text that has been generated by the students themselves (a report, a list of generalisations, etc).

- Display the text so that all students can see it – or make copies for individuals.

- Select some key content words to delete from the text. The words deleted or covered should be those with which students are familiar.

- Present the text to students with words deleted and ask them to suggest words that could be written in the space in order to make appropriate meaning of the sentence.

- Individuals may be given some time to work on their own and then compare ideas for words with others. There may be several words that are suitable replacements for those deleted.

- With the whole class, work through the text, asking students to provide you with substitute words for those deleted. Check these against the original words. Ask:
    Does the sentence still make sense?
    Is the information conveyed still true?
    What do you think is the best choice of word for this section? Why?

MODIFICATIONS

- The passage can be used to test students' awareness of any scientific or technical language related to the topic. In this case, you may wish to provide more support by revealing first letters, word shapes, and so on.

- The same text can be used with all students, but different words (or number of words) are deleted according to ability level.

- Removable labels can be stuck over text (on a chart or in a big book) and the activity conducted orally.

TEACHING POINTS

- Words generated by students can be used as the starting point of lists exploring various spelling patterns.

Consensus 1–3–6

This is an effective process to help students construct generalisations at the end of a unit. It is also a very good activity for developing negotiation and decision-making skills.

BASIC PROCEDURE

- Individually, students generate a list of ideas about the topic. Give students a time limit in which to complete the task and, perhaps, limit the number of items you wish them to list.

- Students now work in groups of three to combine their ideas into one list of statements. Ideas are discussed, modified, justified, included or rejected until a list is agreed upon. Again, a limit on time and the number of statements can assist the process.

- Two trios now get together and repeat the process using the two lists each group has generated. The final list of statements generated by each group of six can be written on large sheets of butchers' paper and displayed for discussion.

MODIFICATIONS

- For younger students – or those less experienced in cooperative work – this procedure can be done using 1–2 or 1–2–4 groupings.

- Individual lists can be retained by the teacher for assessment purposes.

TEACHING POINTS

- Encourage students to reflect on the process of coming to a consensus.

- Follow the activity by asking each group to prioritise their ideas.

- Compare statements to those made at the beginning of the unit.

Cross-impact grid

This is an interesting way in which students can explore the relationships between trends or events in a particular topic. (Derived from idea in Pike & Selby 1988.)

BASIC PROCEDURE

- You need to test your topic for its appropriateness to this strategy. List items, events or trends that have been explored and consider whether they have an impact on each other in some way. If so, then this strategy may be useful.

- Draw up a grid. Along the top row, write a series of events or trends.

- Write the same items in the first column.

- Students then fill the grid in by analysing the relationship between each combination of items – how each impacts on the other. For example, for a topic 'Let's not say goodbye', students consider the relationship between some of the causes of endangered species:

	Habitat loss	Hunting/poaching	Pollution
Habitat loss	X	Less habitat means animals located in more confined space. More vulnerable to poachers. Easier to police?	Loss of vegetation means less available to clean the air. Less defence against pollution.
Hunting/poaching	Not much effect on habitat unless habitat is cleared for hunting purposes	X	Some forms of hunting can pollute the environment (eg lead from shooting, poison from baiting).
Pollution	Pollution has direct impact on habitat loss, eg: water pollution, loss of habitat for frogs.	Pollution has indirect impact on hunting. Fewer animals to hunt.	X

MODIFICATIONS

- Students could come up with their own list of items for the grid.

- Newspaper articles that explore an issue involving future developments can be used as the basis for the activity.

TEACHING POINTS

- This activity can be combined with effects wheels as it requires similar thinking. Some of the items generated by an effects wheel could be analysed within a cross-impact grid.

Crossword puzzles

Students work with a familiar and fun activity in order to present their understanding of a topic to others.

BASIC PROCEDURE

- This activity assumes that students have some knowledge and experience of doing crossword puzzles. It is worth spending some time looking at crosswords – how they are presented and how the clues are worded.

- This activity requires students to create their own puzzle and to devise all the clues.

- Individually, students develop a list of words based on what they have learned about the topic.

- The lists should be checked for relevance and correct spelling.

- Students then work at organising the words into crossword form. This is more easily done if they are given a prepared grid to experiment with.

- Once they have established a position for each word, they then devise a set of clues for 'across' and 'down'.

- The crosswords are then drawn up neatly and shared among the class.

MODIFICATIONS

- Some computer software has crossword-making programs.

TEACHING POINTS

- The important thing is that students have the responsibility of devising the clues. It is this aspect of the activity that will challenge them to draw on what they know.

Diamond display

In this activity, students must think about what they consider to be most important or most true to them about a topic. It is a useful way to explore the personal values and perspectives that have emerged through an investigation.

BASIC PROCEDURE

- Prepare a set of nine statements of opinion related to your topic. The statements should vary in point of view and, if possible, incorporate various generalisations that the students have made themselves during the unit.

- The statements can be written on a sheet, each one in a box to be cut out by the student.

- Read the sheet of statements with students, making sure they understand the meaning of each one Each student cuts out their set of statements.

- Students are asked to arrange the statements into a diamond shape:

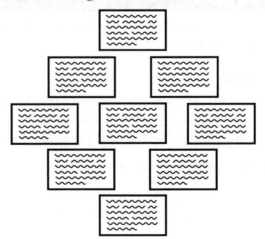

- The statement at the top of the diamond is the one they most agree with. Other statements are placed in order of priority until the last statement at the bottom is placed – the one with which they least agree.

- Pairs and trios then share their diamond displays, justifying their choices as appropriate.

MODIFICATIONS

- The activity can be simplified by using fewer statements and changing the shape students must make. For example, four statements could simply be organised into a single line – from *agree with most* to *agree with least*.

- Some unit topics may not lend themselves well to statements of opinion. Factual information can also be organised in this way according to how 'true' students believe each statement to be.

- Statements can also be hung around or pinned to nine students. Others then take it in turns to organise them into a diamond shape.

TEACHING POINTS

- This is best carried out as an individual activity. It gives students the opportunity to reflect on their own points of view and understandings in relation to a topic.

- Encourage students to discuss the way they have organised the statements and to justify their choices. This will provide an insight into their understanding about the topic.

De Bono's 6 thinking hats

This strategy can serve many different purposes and be applied to a range of contexts. It has been suggested under the making-conclusions stage of a unit because it is particularly effective when students have some knowledge of a topic to bring to the task. This is an excellent way to recap and bring together some of the key perspectives from the unit, and helps to develop the students' thinking skills.

BASIC PROCEDURE

- **Red hat** represents feelings and emotions: *How do you feel about this issue?*
- **White hat** represents facts: *What do we know to be true about this issue? What are the facts?*
- **Yellow hat** represents the positives: *What are all the benefits? positive outcomes?*
- **Black hat** represents the negatives: *What are the disadvantages? negative outcomes?*
- **Green hat** represents creativity: *What are some solutions or alternatives?*
- **Blue hat** represents thinking about thinking: *What is this issue really all about? What are some of the main themes? What has it made you think about?*

- Introduce the nature of each of the six thinking hats one at a time and practise using the hat in response to issues and events throughout the day.

For example: *What would a 'black hat thinker' say to this? Let's put our red hats on after that story ... how do you feel?*

- Once students are familiar with the nature of each hat, they can use them in all sorts of ways. Try giving different groups a different color. That group must respond to an issue, question or problem according to that hat's perspective. They document their idea on large sheets of paper.

- The sheets of paper are passed on until every group has written something down. A new idea is added to each sheet.

- Students are asked to think about the hat they most and least identify with and why.

MODIFICATIONS

- Use actual colored hats to help the activity become more concrete. Try making a set of paper hats that can be used at any time during the day.

- Develop characters for role-play around the ideas generated from the 6 hats activities.

- Draw, paint or mime responses using the hats as a guide.

- Organise the students into groups of six to discuss the topic. Each group has a set of six colored hats. The hats are rotated around the group and each person must comment accordingly.

TEACHING POINTS

- The 6 thinking hats can be used to help solve a range of day-to-day problems. Encourage students to consider their preferred hat/s. Do they tend to use a 'black hat' approach to solving problems? The technique can be applied to evaluating the effectiveness of group work and other procedures.

- Ask students to consider other hats that people wear when responding to issues relating to others (eg gender bias, thoughtful of others, impulsive). Assign new colors to your hats.

Effects wheels

Effects wheels (also called consequence wheels or futures wheels) are a wonderful strategy for helping students think laterally about a topic and for considering the implications of some of the issues arising from it. This is a very useful way of reinforcing the concept of cause and effect, and is also used as a decision-making tool.

BASIC PROCEDURE

- Model an effects wheel to students based around a familiar topic (eg 'more homework' or 'buying a pet'). Demonstrate the ways in which each consequence leads to another.

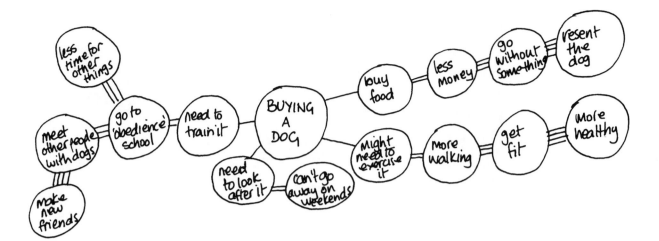

- Select an issue or event pertinent to the topic being investigated and ask students to work individually or in pairs to construct their own effects wheel.

- Ask students to develop statements of generalisation based on the information in their effects wheel.

MODIFICATIONS

- For younger students, model the procedure showing only one or two layers of consequences.

- A giant 'effects' wheel can be constructed on one wall of the classroom and added to throughout the unit.

- Students can add causes to their effects wheels using arrows to show the difference between cause and effect.

TEACHING POINTS

- When used at this stage in the unit, effects wheels are a very effective assessment strategy for determining the degree to which a student has made connections within a topic.

- Effects wheels can also be a useful way of exploring the possible outcomes of actions the student may want to take as a result of their learning in a unit.

- The task is also a useful tool for teaching the language of explanation: *If ... then* .... Students can be encouraged to write a series of cause and effect statements from their own maps or to interpret the maps others make.

A year 1 class display of the consequences of losing grasslands.

In my club

This is a version of the basic concept attainment technique. It is a useful strategy at the end of the unit as it helps you to assess the extent to which students have understood the concepts embedded in your unit topic. It also provides students with the opportunity to make links between concepts they have attained.

BASIC PROCEDURE

- Choose a concept central to the unit you have been exploring – rainforest, invertebrates, government …

- Draw a simple 'yes/no' table on the chalkboard.

Yes	No

- Provide students with example/s of words associated with the chosen key concept. For example, words such as *vine, water,* and *darkness* could be associated with the key concept of 'forest'.

- Ask students to deduce the key concept by suggesting their own words. If their guesses are associated with the key concept, they are placed in the 'yes' column; if they are unassociated with the key concept they are placed in the 'no' column. This step is repeated until the key concept is deduced.

Meat eaters and non-meat eaters

Yes	No
dog	horse
cat	kangaroo
snake	wombat

MODIFICATIONS

- Pictures placed in each column are an effective way of using this strategy with young children.

- You can be as specific or general as you wish in this activity. You may decide to narrow the field using two or three criteria for the 'yes' column. For example, for a topic on animals, the 'yes' column might only accept animals without a backbone that live underground.

- Once students become familiar with the game, they can use their own knowledge of the topic to create 'In my club' games for each other.

TEACHING POINTS

- Ask children not to identify the criteria for the game once they have guessed it. The aim is to have as many students 'on board' as possible, not to be the first to guess. Students who have worked it out can help others by suggesting more words for each column.

Laying it on the line

This is a delightful activity – motivating for all age groups. Importantly, it helps students to make conclusions not only about what they know, but also about what they value and feel in relation to the topic. This can be done as an oral or written activity – or the two can be combined. This activity helps develop confidence in stating and justifying opinions.

BASIC PROCEDURE

- Prepare four signs reading: strongly disagree, disagree, agree, strongly agree. These can be placed in four corners or along a line. The 'line' could be a piece of string held by two students.

- Read out a statement relating to the topic, to which students must respond by placing themselves along a line according to the extent to which they agree or disagree.

- Once students have moved to their preferred position, conduct some 'on the spot' interviews with them, asking them to explain why they have chosen that position.

- After the activity, ask students to comment on the way they felt having to make decisions about 'where they stood', for example: pressure to stand where they friends were, uncertainty about the topic or issue, or uncertainty about their own beliefs.

- Ask students to reflect on what the activity has taught them.
    Why do we think about things so differently from one another?
    How do our beliefs and values influence our decisions and actions?
    How and why do our values change?
    Why have we come to think this way about this topic?

MODIFICATIONS

- This activity can also be carried out in written form. Write the statements on a page and ask student to indicate where they stand along a line beneath the statement.

- For young students, symbols such as smiley, neutral and sad faces could be used to indicate yes, not sure and no.

- Once students are familiar with the strategy, they can design their own statements to read out to the class.

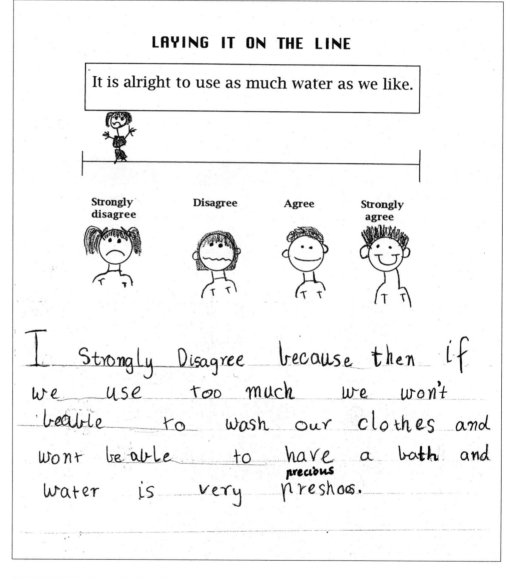

Lauren's opinion about water use at the end of a unit of work (year 1).

TEACHING POINTS

- The interviews that accompany this activity are important. It is by justifying why they have chosen to position themselves at a certain point along the line that students reveal most about what they have learned and how they feel. Use a microphone (it need not be a real one) to interview the students. Hamming up the activity takes the pressure off.

- It is important to stress to students that there is no right or wrong position to stand in. This activity is about personal opinions and these should be respected.

Learning maps

Students create a map of their learning throughout the unit. Like a story map, it shows in pictures and written text, various key 'scenes' from the unit. Students are also asked to reflect on the success of their learning in each activity.

BASIC PROCEDURE

- Gather the class together and discuss the unit of work that has been completed. Ask students to recall the activities covered. Memories can be jogged by rereading learning logs, looking at displays around the room, and so on.

- Ask students, in pairs or individually, to draw the journey of the unit as they might a story map. The maps should be sequential, showing pictures of the various activities in which the student has been engaged.

- Encourage students to write a brief recount (if appropriate) of the various activities in which they were involved. Speech balloons and captions should be used to help explain the pictures.

- Now ask students to annotate their maps with some reflective comments about how they felt about the activities, which sections of the unit they liked most and least and why, and so on.

- Share the maps and note differences and similarities among various perceptions of the unit.

MODIFICATIONS

- There are numerous alternatives to this basic idea. A whole-class learning map can be constructed during or at the end of the unit. Groups can be responsible for depicting certain scenes from the unit, and writing a caption and a reflective comment.

- You may prefer to provide children with an outline of the map with certain activities labelled – the focus then becomes the reflective comment rather than remembering all the activities.

- Photographs that have been taken throughout the unit can also be used to construct a whole class representation.

TEACHING POINTS

- If students have kept a learning log (see chapter 7) during the unit, it will be a helpful reference for them when completing this activity.

- The strategy needs to be carefully modelled if students have never attempted it before. Start with a simple story map based on a familiar book to introduce them to the task.

- Spend time sharing the learning maps and discuss why there are differences in the way we respond to activities. Student should use the maps to analyse for themselves what kinds of learning situations are the most effective for them.

- Learning maps are a wonderful way to share the results of your unit with parents and the general school community. Show them off!

Similes and metaphors

By exploring similes or metaphors for the topic they have been exploring, students will demonstrate the degree to which they understand what the topic both is and is not about.

BASIC PROCEDURE

- There are many ways that similes and metaphors can be used in teaching. For this stage of a unit, you may wish to provide students with a simile to explore, for example:

  We have been finding out all about the planet Earth. I want you to think about what you know about the human body [studied in a previous unit]. How is the Earth like a human body?

  or ask students to invent their own similes:

  We have been finding out all about families. What are some other things that remind you of families? Why? A family is like a ... because ...

- This activity works best in small groups – or even as a whole-class brainstorm.

MODIFICATIONS

- Ask students to list ways in which the chosen simile is both like and not like the topic.

TEACHING POINTS

- If students are unfamiliar with this technique, begin by providing metaphors for familiar topics and practise exploring the links between them. For example, you could ask students:

  How is our school like a circus?
  How is moving to a new grade like bungee jumping?
  How is growing up like a journey?

- Look for evidence of the use of simile and metaphor in books and other resource material.

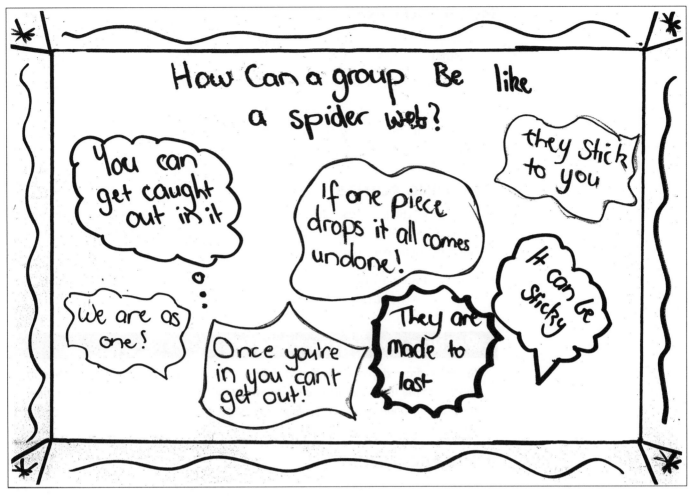

Using the idea of a spider web as a simile for a group.

PMI: plus–minus–interesting to see

By analysing an event or issue using this simple structure, students can be helped to see the 'bigger picture'. (From De Bono 1976.)

BASIC PROCEDURE

- Select a 'What if' statement that is related to the topic (and understandings) being studied. For example:

  What if all world leaders were women? (from a unit on leadership)

  What if life was discovered on Mars? (from a unit on space)

  What if all people had the same colored skin? (from a unit of work on cultural diversity)

- Brainstorm the issues arising from this possibility under the three headings:

  plus – focusing on perceived positive outcomes

  minus – focusing on perceived negative outcomes

  interesting to see – issues, questions and possibilities that arise from the idea

MODIFICATIONS

- This activity can be done as a quick, whole-class exercise, individually or in small groups.

- Students responses could be written, drawn, acted or reported orally.

- Once students are familiar with the technique, they can work in trios, each taking it in turns to come up with as many ideas in each category as they can.

TEACHING POINTS

- It can be difficult for some students to come up with responses in the categories that go against their personal beliefs. Sometimes, combining the strategy with role-play helps here.

- The strategy can be a useful precursor to formal debate and can also help students write a persuasive text.

Putting you in the picture

Students draw a picture within a frame, showing how they see themselves in relation to the topic they have been investigating. This encourages students to think more deeply about their own feelings, values, attitudes and actions in relation to the topic.

BASIC PROCEDURE

- Give students a simple outline of a picture frame, or ask them to draw one on the page.

- Ask students to think about the topic they have been exploring and all the things they have learnt. Now ask: *What has this got to do with you? Where do you fit into the picture?*

- Students then draw, write or map their ideas about the connections between the topic and themselves.

- Share frames with others and display them, gallery style, around the classroom.

MODIFICATIONS

- Students may prefer to write a summary statement or even a set of words inside the frame.

- Groups of students could use the 'freeze frame' device (see page 68) to show how they see themselves in relation to the topic.

- Make a large frame using cardboard. Students take turns to hold the frame around their face and then present an oral summary of what they have learned to the class.

TEACHING POINTS

- This activity is best presented in a very open-ended format. Allow students to show you what they can do.

- The following questions can work as prompts:
  When you see yourself doing something about this topic, what do you see? Draw your imagined picture.
  How do you feel about what we have learned? Draw your feeling.

Question ball

A large, plastic ball covered in focus questions is thrown from student to student. Each student must answer a question before throwing on.

BASIC PROCEDURE

- Purchase a large, light, plastic ball. Write a series of questions on sticky labels (write each question in a different color). The questions should prompt students to make statements about the understandings they have gained from the unit. Attach the labels to the ball.

- Throw the ball to around the room. When a student catches it, call out a color.

- The student must answer the question written in that color.

- The ball is then thrown to another student, and so on.

MODIFICATIONS

- Instead of questions, you could use words (students use the word in a sentence), pictures (students tell you something they know about the picture), or sentence beginnings for students to complete. You could even write answers on the ball to which the students must provide questions.

- The same activity can be done using a cube made from cardboard and rolled along the floor like a dice.

TEACHING POINTS

- Establish some clear rules for this activity, such as alternating between girls and boys for each throw.

- If questions are open ended, the same question can be answered many different ways by different students.

- Students can create their own questions for the ball.

- The sticky labels enable you to reuse the ball for another unit

Question me an answer

This activity requires students to come up with questions for answers. This is an excellent activity for developing questioning skills.

BASIC PROCEDURE

- Select a set of key words that are central to the unit understandings.

- Tell students that they must devise a question for which each word would be the answer, for example:

  The word is 'oxygen'. What is the question? [What is something that animals need in order to survive?]

- Students share their questions. For some words, several questions will be acceptable. For others (those that deal with straightforward, factual information) there will be fewer variations of questions.

- The activity can be turned into a game by having pairs of students come out to the front. The first student to come up with an acceptable question wins and is then challenged by the next student.

MODIFICATIONS

- Another way of applying the same strategy is to provide half the students with questions (each student has a question on a strip of paper) and half the students with an answer.

  - Students must then move around the room and match questions with answers.

  - They sit down when they have found a match.

  - The activity continues until all students are seated.

- The activity can also be done orally. Students work in pairs and conduct 'backwards interviews' where the answer is said before the questions. Backwards interviews can be performed to the rest of the class.

TEACHING POINTS

- If students are new to this activity, a good way to introduce it is to read a picture story book and then use the answer/question technique to revise the key events or ideas in the book.

Statements of generalisation

Students write statements, summarising what they have learned during the unit. (See also Consensus 1–3–6.)

BASIC PROCEDURE

- Ask students to spend some time reflecting on what they have learned during the investigation.

- Each student then writes a set of statements under the heading: *What I now know about ... [the topic].*

- Statements are displayed, discussed, challenged, compared and modified.

MODIFICATIONS

- Students can cut their statements up into words and exchange with a partner to reconstruct.

- Each student could write one statement to contribute to a class list.

- The teacher could scribe for students.

- Students are given a set of key words about which they must write a statement, for example:

  Write some statements about machines. Use these words to help you: work, materials, parts, household, energy, force.

TEACHING POINTS

- Generalisations should be compared with any generated at the beginning of the unit. Encourage students to comment on the way their ideas have changed.

- Some students find it difficult to write a generalisation as opposed to a fact. Giving them key words to write about (particularly concept words) helps here.

- Compare the statements with your own set of understandings planned at the beginning of the unit. You could also share these with the students.

> **Different animals eat different food.**
> Dogs eat bones and meat.
> Cats eat fish.
> Rabbits eat carrots and lettuce.
> Guinea pigs eat carrots and lettuce.
> Birds eat seeds.

Five-year-olds generalise about animals.

Two trues and a false

This activity can be used as a quick quiz at the end of a unit and is a fun way to ascertain the extent to which students have retained important factual information related to the topic.

BASIC PROCEDURE

- Devise approximately ten sets of statements. In each set, you need three statements, two of which are true and one which is false. For example, for a topic on insects, one set of statements could be:

  All insects have three body parts. (true)
  All insects have 6 legs. (true)
  All insects fly. (false)

- Ask students to prepare a sheet for their answers. They write the numbers 1 to 3 in ten sections on their page. Explain that you will be reading sets of three statements and that, each time, one statement out of the three will be false

- Read out the sets of statements. Students must write the letter T if they think it is true or F if they think it is false. Once they have made a decision, they cannot change it.

- Work through each set of statements and then ask students to share their responses.

- Once the students have got the idea, they can prepare a set of 'two trues and a false' to challenge other class members.

MODIFICATIONS

- You may choose to read out all the statements in a set before students mark down their true and false selection. This provides them with more information and support.

TEACHING POINTS

- This activity is only effective with factual information about a topic. Use data that has been collected by the students themselves

Time capsules

The choice of items for a topic-based time capsule can be a fascinating insight into what students have learned about a topic.

BASIC PROCEDURE

- This activity involves students in creating a time capsule of items relating to the topic being studied.

- Ask students to consider the question:
  If you were to choose five items to put in a container that would represent the important things we know about … [the topic], what would they be?

- Explain that their task is to try to show the people of the future what they understood about the topic at this point in history.

- Students can work alone or in teams to design or create their time capsule.

- Ideas are shared. If desired, the 'top five' items from across the class can then be selected for a single capsule to represent the class.

- Items are then placed in a container and buried somewhere in or around the school grounds for future generations to discover.

MODIFICATIONS

- The time capsule could be created literally (actually putting items in a sealed container and burying it somewhere for future discovery) or students could draw the items they would include.

- By simply designing rather than actually creating the capsule, students will have more scope in their selection of items.

- Ask students to think about what a time capsule from 50 years ago might have contained for the same topic. Or imagine what could be included in 50 years' time.

TEACHING POINTS

- This activity is a useful way of exploring the way our knowledge base changes over time; and seeing that many of the things we now know about the world will be proved wrong in the years to come.

- Discuss some of the views about the world that have been radically changed over time: that the world is flat; that smoking is harmless, and so on.

What am I?

This is a favorite game with teachers and students alike. It is more effectively placed at the end of a unit because it enables students to use their accumulated knowledge. Combining it with the activity of moving around the room can be a refreshing change of pace for students.

BASIC PROCEDURE

- Prepare a set of sticky labels, each one depicting an item linked to your topic.

- Seat students in a circle and place stickers on their backs so they cannot see their own, but they can clearly see others'.

- Remind students that they are not to tell each other what the item is.

- Students then move around the room asking each other 'yes/no' questions, to try to and work out their particular item.

- Once they have worked it out, the sticker is removed.

- Students continue as part of the game – answering questions until everyone has identified their item.

MODIFICATIONS

- Pictures could be used instead of words. Paste pictures to card and use safety pins to attach the cards to students' backs.

- The words can also be written on strips of card and then made into a headband.

- Once students have identified their item, they are then asked to organise themselves into a groups. For example: *Can you find other people with labels that belong with yours?*

- The activity can be modified by having a panel of students facing the class, each with a label attached to a headband. The panel then asks yes/no questions of the whole class, until they guess their identity. A new panel is then created.

TEACHING POINTS

- If students are unfamiliar with this activity, they will need some instruction on asking appropriate questions. All questions should have either a 'yes' or 'no' answer. Most will begin with: *Can I ..., Have I ..., Do I ...?*, etc.

6 STRATEGIES

for taking action

BROAD PURPOSES

- to assist students to make links between their understandings and their experience in the real world
- to enable students to make choices and develop the belief that they can be effective participants in society
- to provide further insight into students' understandings for future unit planning
- to reinforce the link between school, home and the wider community
- to provide further opportunities and contexts for ongoing learning about the topic

About this stage of a unit

While taking action is presented here as the final stage in a unit, students can initiate action in response to their learning at any time. Indeed, the action taken might, in itself, be a source of information. However, strategies to assist students in acting on their learning have been identified as the final stage because they allow students to apply what they have learned through their investigation to a real-life, purposeful context. This is also an important part of the assessment of students' learning – the willingness and ability to apply their learning in a practical way tells us much about what students have gained from a unit.

Strategies for action will be appropriate for some units more than others. When topics selected are meaningful and relevant to the lives of students, and their local or global community and environment, there is almost always some way they can make some contribution to change.

'Taking action' is an important part of integrated learning because it demonstrates to students the relevance and purpose of what they have been investigating. Ideally, the desire to take action should arise within the students themselves and be subsequently owned by them. Too many well-intended action programs in schools are short lived; they must emerge as part of the process of investigating and understanding the world around us. Action should be empowering – it should help students see the way they can make a difference to their own lives or the lives of others.

The term 'action' often brings to mind images of rallies, demonstrations and people chained to bulldozers. Whilst such forms of action have a role in influencing change, they are indeed inappropriate for young students. Strategies for action should be concerned with the immediate and tangible. The home, family, neighborhood, school grounds and local community offer a rich array of possibilities for exploration and action. Actions should be things that students themselves can actually do and, ideally, something from which they see a real outcome. Building a compost heap, caring for a classroom pet or devising a code of behavior for the school ground are all ways in which students can apply their learning about the world to everyday life.

Most strategies for action will be very specific to the topic being studied. They will emerge in the particular context in which your students live, and relate to the needs in and around your particular community. Some examples of these specific action outcomes include:

- At the end of a unit of work on energy, students could decide to bring hand towels to school rather than using paper towels, or make signs to remind people to switch lights off when leaving the room.

- At the end of a unit of work on waste and recycling, students may decide to bring lunch and play lunch in reusable containers, avoid throw-away wrappers, and set up a compost system in the school grounds.

While many ideas for action will emerge from the students themselves, it is a good idea to consider possibilities for action as you plan the unit. Your role will be to support students in the process and make suggestions that are feasible and achievable. At this point in a unit, the following questions will be useful. These questions can be worked through as a class, in small groups or individually. You will be surprised at how inventive young learners will be when given the opportunity to consider ways they can make a difference:

> *Now that we have found out more about this topic, what are we concerned about?*
> *Why are we concerned about it?*
> *What is already being done about it?*
> *What are some of the things we think need to be done? (at home, at school, in the neighborhood, the world*
> *Which of these things can we do or convince others to do?*
> *What steps will we need to take to implement the action?*
> *What jobs need to be done and who will do them?*
> *What resources/equipment will we need?*
> *Whom do we need to talk to about this? Do we need to seek permission?*
> *What difficulties do we think might arise?*
> *What can we do to help prevent these?*
> *How will we know whether our action has been effective?*

When designing strategies for taking action, our aim should be to help students feel they have made a positive and constructive contribution to change. Therefore, it is important that the action is appropriate to their age and capabilities. The strategies in this chapter can be used for a range of topics and contexts.

Advertising campaigns

Students use persuasive techniques of advertising to encourage others to take action.

BASIC PROCEDURE

- Begin by discussing some of the more successful advertising campaigns students know. What ads do they remember best? Why?

- View and listen to television, radio and magazine advertisements. List the techniques used to persuade people to buy a product or change their behavior.

- Consider ways in which others could be informed or persuaded through advertising related to the issue you have explored.

- Discuss the key issues related to your topic: *What message do we want to get across?*

- Some of the methods students could use to create an advertisement include making posters, writing jingles, devising slogans, making pamphlets, using music and oral language for radio advertisements, and creating television-style ads on video.

- Advertisements are then shown to other students, displayed around the school or community or included in the newspaper (see above) or newsletter.

MODIFICATIONS

- Use an existing advertisement as the 'template' for your own. Change the content but use the same techniques. For example, students could use the melody of a McDonald's advertising jingle and change the words to advertise the importance of eating healthy food.

TEACHING POINTS

- This strategy for action works best when students bring to it some understanding of the nature of advertising. This could be explored as a unit topic in itself or may be the focus of a parallel English/arts unit on persuasive language and images.

- If possible, invite someone involved in the advertising industry to talk to students about effective methods.

Annotated exhibitions

By sharing work done throughout the unit, students can inform others about the issues central to the topic. At the same time, they will be reflecting on their own learning.

BASIC PROCEDURE

- Gather students together and construct a list of the activities they have done throughout the unit of work (see 'Learning maps, page 113).

- Explain to students that they are going to turn the classroom into an exhibition centre or gallery so their learning can be shared with others.

- Select key pieces of work and resources used throughout the unit, and display them in sequential order around the classroom. Students could mount particular work samples so they are more effectively presented to others.

- Organise groups of students to write captions explaining the significance of various items around the room. Younger students could suggest captions for each item and have you scribe them.

- Compile a 'catalogue of exhibits' – numbering each one – to help visitors make their way around the room.

- Send out invitations to parents and friends.

- Have a grand opening!

MODIFICATIONS

- The same idea can be used to present one aspect of the unit rather than work from throughout the investigation. For example, models made at the sorting-out phase of the unit might become the focus of an informative exhibition.

- Small groups of students can be made responsible for designing an exhibit to explain an aspect of the topic for others. The exhibit is then created and displayed.

TEACHING POINTS

- Students can act as gallery guides and show visitors through the exhibition.

- If possible, you could find it easier to use another room for the exhibition and organise specific viewing times.

- Make sure the captions explain what the work sample is and why it was done

- Invite visitors to fill in a visitors book, commenting on what they have learned from the exhibition

Arts in the local community

Visual or performing art works in and around the local community can be a powerful way to share information or persuade others to act. This is also a wonderful boost to students' self-esteem.

BASIC PROCEDURE

- Make sure you have investigated, prior to this strategy, possible sites where art works may be displayed or performed, for example local shopping centres, banks, community centres, and council buildings.

- Discuss with students what they regard as the most important things they have learned from their investigation.

- Ask students: *What do you think is important for other people in the community to know about this?*

- If appropriate, students can work with you to seek permission for the display of art works in the local community by writing letters or making phone calls.

- Using either art works already completed (as part of the sorting-out process) or new works designed for the purpose, choose what will be displayed or performed. Captions explaining the significance of the pieces should be included.

- If possible, involve students in helping set up the display area.

MODIFICATIONS

- A similar display could be created in a public area of the school, informing parents and others.

TEACHING POINTS

- Make sure that displayed work is deserving of publication. Students should understand the importance of correct spelling and overall presentation to the public.

- If possible, include a visitors book or response sheet in the area so people can provide feedback to the students.

- Place a notice in the newsletter telling parents about the work on display.

Designing self-guided walks

This is particularly appropriate for environmental topics.

BASIC PROCEDURE

- Discuss the concept of a self-guided walk or trail. Basically, students will be mapping out a route for others to take, using specific sites along the way to help explain more about the topic.

- Consider a route that could be used for a walk or trail to inform people about what has been learned as a result of your unit. Examples include:

  For a housing unit: a walk to show different styles or eras

  For a unit dealing with cultural diversity: a local walk to point out the way various cultures have influenced the neighborhood

  For a unit on plants: a school ground trail showing different plants, how they should be cared for, when they flower, etc

  For a unit on advertising: a walk to show people how prevalent visual advertising is in the local area

  For a unit on local history: a walk to show historical sites of significance in the neighborhood

  For a unit of work on structures: a walk to show various structures in and around the school and how they are made

- If necessary, take students on a guided walk in the local area to show them how such a walk is structured. (This may already have been done at the finding-out stage.) Collect examples of guides from places like the tourist bureau, conservation department, local council and historical society.

- If possible, visit the site you will be using as the basis for the walk and take photographs of the areas students wish to highlight.

- Now design a map and guide sheet or brochure that people will use as a guide to the walk. Pairs of students could be responsible for describing the significance of particular sites along the way.

- Publish the maps and guide sheets and make them available to parents and friends in the local community. (This could also be a fund-raising activity.)

MODIFICATIONS

- Instead of a written guide to the walk, students make an audio tape that people listen to as they walk or drive around the chosen route.

- The activity could be completed on a small scale, and focus on the area in and around the school. Pairs of students can design trails for others in the class.

- Interpretive signs can be made to accompany significant points in the trail, but this is only feasible in the school-ground context.

TEACHING POINTS

- This activity combines mathematics (mapping), language, art and graphic communication. It could be a class project that begins at the finding-out stage – where students are taken to the site as a shared experience – and continued throughout the unit.

- A video or photographic record of the main sites of significance along the walk can help the construction of the guide back in the classroom.

- Invite people to write to the class to share their responses to the walk.

Develop an action plan for the school

Bringing about change within the school context can be a very effective form of action because it is immediate and relevant to the students, and the experience will often demonstrate the problems associated with implementing change in the wider community.

BASIC PROCEDURE

- The procedure used will depend very much on the nature of the action students wish to take. Some examples of possible action emerging from various units of work include:
  - improving access to the school for people with disabilities
  - reducing bullying behaviors in the school ground
  - reducing packaging for products sold in the canteen
  - changing something in relation to the uniform code
  - improving an area of the school ground

- While the processes students go through to implement their desired action will vary, there are some basic steps that may be helpful.

- Ensure that all students are clear about what outcome they wish to see as a result of their actions.

- Brainstorm all the different ways that outcome could be reached.

- List the things that are likely to help and hinder the process.

- List the key people who will need to be persuaded or those who will be most affected by this change.

- Consider resources that might be needed and how these will be obtained.

- Consider a timeline for the process.

- Allocate roles and tasks to various members of the class.

- As part of the process, students may need to:
  - address a school assembly to explain their plan
  - write a report for the school newsletter
  - survey parents, students and staff to gather support
  - appear at the school or student council meeting to outline their proposal

- Consider the ways in which the effectiveness of the action will be monitored. A trial period could be put in place, after which the action will be reviewed.

MODIFICATIONS

- The sample process can be followed to implement a small-scale action in the classroom (eg a new system for managing shared classroom resources, or a new system for dealing with inappropriate behavior).

- The process could be carried out by a small group of students as a special project.

TEACHING POINTS

- The process of bringing about some kind of change in the school provides many opportunities for teaching across the curriculum. Writing letters, designing petitions, present oral arguments, lobbying and decision-making are just some of the skills that students might be using during this process.

- Make these skills explicit as you work with students. Compare what they are doing with any current local or global issues in which a group of people are working to bring about change.

From here to there

This is a useful way to help students plan a course of action. It is best done in conjunction with one of the action procedures outlined below.

BASIC PROCEDURE

- Clear a large display area – either a pinboard, whiteboard or chalk board – on which students will be able to display their ideas.

- Discuss what the current 'state of play' is in relation to your issue. Draw or write about this current state of play and display these ideas at one end of the display space under the heading 'Here'.

- At the other end of the display space, place the heading 'There' and ask students to draw or write their ideas about what they would like to see changed.

- Now ask students to consider what needs to be done to get from 'here' to 'there'. In groups, they discuss possible steps along the way, write or draw their ideas, and place them along the path between the two ends of the display.

- Come together as a class and share the suggestions. Place the suggestions in order, according to what should be done first, second, and so on. If possible, create a timeline for the process.

- Now you have the beginnings of an action plan.

MODIFICATIONS

- Students could use this techniques to come up with their own or a small-group action plan.

- A flowchart rather than timeline might be the preferred form of display.

TEACHING POINTS

- This strategy can be effectively managed by giving students a set of index cards on which they write or draw their ideas. They then pin their cards to the display space.

Global links

Communication technology holds great potential for students to make links with other people around the world who are involved in action projects.

BASIC PROCEDURE

- There is no specific format for developing this kind of action strategy. It will depend on the issue and whether or not action programs are being recorded on, for example, the Internet.

- If you have access to the Internet, search for your topic – particularly within the broader domain of education.

- Information can then be shared between students and others involved in action projects around the world. This is often in the form of entering data gathered in a 'global bank' on the issue. Examples of such global programs include monitoring water quality, national and international bird observation and tallying, and tree conservation measures.

MODIFICATIONS

- Older students could begin their own campaign to create a site to which others contribute information and ideas. Set up your own home page and invite visitors to help consider appropriate local and global action.

TEACHING POINTS

- Naturally, the use of the Internet as a form of action is limited by the access your school has to the appropriate technology and the students' own experience. There may, however, be students who have the access at home and could work through this as individuals on behalf of the class.

- Be aware of the potential for bogus sites to raise money or involve students in spurious schemes. It is important to keep a watchful eye on the sites discovered and communications made.

- If possible, link up with other schools around the world to discuss what you have learned about the topic and to compare notes.

Hear all about it

This involves creating a news program for 'radio' or 'television'.

BASIC PROCEDURE

- Follow the same guidelines for creating a newspaper to create a news broadcast related to the topic. (See 'Read all about it' page XX.) The program can be taped and 'aired' to the school community or performed live. Again, it may include experts from activities already conducted in the unit (interviews, role-plays, etc).

Letter writing

Students may wish to register a protest against or their support for a particular issue based on their investigations during a topic. Letters can be written to individuals, organisations or specific newspapers or magazines. The activity of letter writing should be something that arises from the students rather than being dictated by teachers.

BASIC PROCEDURE

- Help students with the process by ensuring that they know to whom the letter is best directed.

- If necessary, model a structure for letter writing, showing students the correct conventions for greetings, signing off, addressing the letter and so on.

- Work through the letter as you would any piece of writing that is to be published. It is important that students work on the presentation of the letter so their message is not clouded by poor attention to spelling, grammar or handwriting.

- Include self-addressed and stamped envelopes to encourage the recipient to reply.

MODIFICATIONS

- A whole-class letter could be written jointly.

TEACHING POINTS

- You may need to explain the process or seek permission from parents before students write to individuals or organisations.

- Explain to students that many organisations and individuals receive hundreds of letters a day and it may be a long time before they receive a reply – if they receive one at all. Action on a more abstract, global scale can also be effective. Usually this takes the form of such things as letters to politicians or newspapers. Whilst we should alert students to this form of action, we need to be sensitive to the possibility that students may not get an immediate response or any response at all and that this can be a disempowering experience.

Meet the press

Invite the local paper to find out all about what you have been investigating. Use the opportunity to inform others.

BASIC PROCEDURE

- Discuss with students ways in which groups and individuals in the community publicise their issues and concerns to others.

- Ask students if they know how some of these stories get onto television or radio news or into the newspaper.

- Consider an event or a product from the unit that could attract the interest of the local media. This may well be combined with another action strategy. For example, you could invite the media to report on the art work you have displayed in the local community.

- If possible, students themselves should contact local media outlets to invite them to interview or visit the school.

MODIFICATIONS

- Contact an organisation that is receiving media attention for their work in the area and inform them about what you are doing. This may be a more effective way of receiving broader media attention.

TEACHING POINTS

- Do some preliminary investigations to find out who the contact people are within local media establishments. This will help streamline the process and avoid frustrating the students' efforts at making contact.

- Make sure that permission is sought from the principal and parents before students are photographed or interviewed.

Personal pledge

Students consider one thing they will do in their own life as a result of what they have learned.

BASIC PROCEDURE

- As a class or individually, brainstorm a list of things that individual students themselves could do in order to act on what they have learned.

- Ask each student to then peruse the list and choose an action that they consider most relevant and achievable to them.

- Each student then writes out a personal pledge, promising to undertake the action within a given time frame.

- Students then read out their pledge to the class.

- One copy of the pledge is taken home and the other is displayed in the classroom.

- The actions incorporated into personal pledges may be very, very simple. It is important that they are achievable. Some examples include:
  - including a new fitness activity into the weekly routine (after a unit of work on healthy bodies)
  - planting a native plant in the garden (after a unit of work on bird life)
  - initiating one fun activity with a younger sibling every week (after a unit of work on families)
- Over the subsequent weeks, ask students to share how easy or difficult it was to put their pledge into action.

MODIFICATIONS

- The class might come up with a shared pledge that each student carries out in their own home environment.
- Present pledges on a fancy 'scroll' for special effect.

TEACHING POINTS

- A letter should be sent home with each student to explain the purpose and significance of the pledge in the context of your integrated unit.
- Give students opportunities to review their pledge if it is becoming more difficult to carry out than anticipated.

Read all about it

To inform others, the class creates a newspaper devoted to the topic.

BASIC PROCEDURE

- Explain to the class that they are going to create a class newspaper to show others what they have learned about during the course of the unit.
- Show students examples of 'single issue' newspapers produced by special interest groups.
- Brainstorm the kinds of things that the newspaper could contain. It might include:
  - the transcript of an interview with a guest speaker from the finding-out stage
  - graphs and survey results from data gathered
  - a report or other text constructed within the unit
  - advertisements persuading readers to consider the issues
  - cartoons and other art works from the unit
  - data boxes including factual information about the topic (Did you know? sections)
  - photographs of various activities students have been involved in

- Allocate responsibilities to various individuals for the production of the paper. You may wish to simulate the roles used in the production of a real newspaper, including editors, chief editor (you!), photographers, cartoonists, reporters, advertising coordinator, and design and layout.

- Once the newspaper is published, celebrate with a launch! It could be sold at a small cost and the money raised donated to a cause relevant to your unit.

MODIFICATIONS

- This may work more effectively as a small group project. It is an excellent enrichment activity for students who require challenge and extension during the unit.

- Consider the use of computer software to help with the layout and design of the newspaper.

- If possible, print copies that can be made available to the local community – at shopping centres and so on.

TEACHING POINTS

- You could alert students to this form of action at the beginning of the unit. In this way, work produced during the unit can be carried out and presented with the newspaper in mind.

- This strategy could be used in conjunction with an English focus on the newspaper or even within a unit on the media itself. Consider inviting someone from the local newspaper to discuss the process. Students should have some prior understanding of the structure and style of a newspaper and the way articles are written and presented.

More strategies for action

In addition to the more detailed strategies outlined above, there are several other ways through which students can take action on issues that concern them. The degree to which these will be appropriate will depend on their availability, relevance to the topic, age of the students and time available.

- Fund raising: activities carried out in order to donate money to a specific cause or to fund an action plan itself (eg to fund the creation of an organic vegetable garden; to buy a compost bin; to sponsor an animal at the zoo; to fund printing costs of pamphlets)

- Publishing picture story books or factual texts to inform other students about the issue

- Making signs around the school (eg to remind people to use water wisely)

- Conducting an audit (of paper used; packaging discarded; use of lights; etc)

- Sponsoring a child in a developing country; an endangered animal; a tree planting project etc

- Creating a student representative council to deal with this and other issues that arise during the year

7

STRATEGIES

for sharing, discussion and reflection

BROAD PURPOSES

- to develop the skills and strategies needed for effective reporting to others
- to analyse the work of other students and provide appropriate, constructive feedback
- to develop in students an understanding of the purposes behind the activities in which they are engaged
- to provide feedback for evaluation purposes about successful and less successful aspects of the unit
- to develop greater understandings of the unit content and the process of inquiry itself
- for students to gain a greater sense of connection between themselves and the unit topic
- to develop positive self-esteem and self-awareness
- to assist students to develop stronger connections between their personal lives and the global domain

About these strategies

Throughout your units of work, students will be required to share ideas with each other, present work to various audiences and reflect on *what* and *how* they are learning. It is as important to extend students' repertoire in these areas as it is to develop their skills of inquiry.

Effective sharing of ideas enables students to learn from each other during a unit. Large and small group discussions are an important forum in which to build a class community. At the same time, students learn skills of turn-taking, questioning, challenging, sharing and so on. Discussions can, however, be less than satisfactory when certain students continue to dominate and others rarely participate. The strategies in this chapter are designed to create more equitable class discussions.

In addition to those for sharing and discussion, strategies for reflection and self-assessment are also included. Like discussions, these strategies should be used throughout a unit of work. Reflection and self-assessment need to be regular, ongoing processes that help the student make sense not only of the unit content but, increasingly, of themselves as learners.

Procedures for the following strategies are summarised to enable you to select them at a glance. There are many more ways to promote discussion, sharing and reflection. You are encouraged to add your own to the suggestions provided.

STRATEGIES FOR SHARING AND DISCUSSION

Carousel sharing

This strategy has the advantage of allowing all groups to share at once and of giving those students in the 'reporting' position a chance to practise their presentation skill several times. This works particularly well as a way of sharing group work products.

BASIC PROCEDURE

- Groups display their work either around their room or on clusters of tables.

- One or two group members are assigned to stay with the display so they can explain the work to others and answer questions.

- Groups then rotate around each of the 'stations' or 'exhibits' – viewing and discussing each other's work.

- The teacher signals the direction in which groups will rotate and indicates the time to move on from each station (using a bell or some other sound).

MODIFICATIONS

- The strategy can be used without stationary reporters. Groups simply rotate around the work products viewing, discussing and interpreting them before a whole-class discussion.

TEACHING POINTS

- Use numbers or colors at each table to help students know where they need to move each time.

- Encourage students who are viewing the work to ask questions and provide feedback on each other's work.

- Use this as a context for assessment of oral reporting skills.

Class meetings

Regular class meetings that use some sort of formal meeting structure can be an excellent way to work through issues, problems or decisions within any unit of work – and, indeed, in relation to class life as a whole.

BASIC PROCEDURE

- If possible, have the students observe a real meeting in progress. It might be a staff meeting held at lunch time or a video of a formal meeting.

- Make a list of some of the strategies and procedures used in meetings and decide on those you wish to adopt. Some useful procedures may include:
  - devising a meeting agenda
  - speaking 'through the chair'
  - establishing a time limit
  - appointing a minute taker

- Appoint a 'chair of the house' whose responsibility is to manage the discussion. This role can rotate so all students have the experience of chairing the meeting.

- Class meetings are probably most relevant at the stage in the unit where students are considering action, and decisions need to be made about what form of action is to be taken.

MODIFICATIONS

- 'Everyone's the teacher'. A much-modified use of this process is simply to nominate different students to manage a discussion about a topic. This develops good questioning skills and can change the climate of a discussion. You become one of the class for the period of the discussion.

TEACHING POINTS

- When students are managing a discussion with groups or the whole class, it can be helpful to work through possible questions to ask and to restate basic rules for whole-class discussion.

Concentric circles

Sometimes called 'donut', this strategy requires students to share ideas with a range of partners.

BASIC PROCEDURE

- Organise two circles of chairs (in equal numbers) facing each other – an outer and inner circle.

- Students take up position on the chairs. Each student sits facing a partner.

- The pairs discuss a given question, topic, problem or experience. At a given signal, those in the outer circle move one chair to the right and discuss their ideas with a new partner.

- Continue the rotation until it seems appropriate to pause for a whole class reflection on what has been learned.

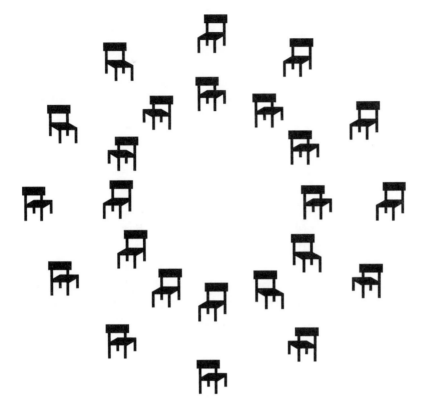

MODIFICATIONS

- The strategy can be made more challenging by having students report to their new partner what they have been told by their previous partner. They then move to the next person and repeat the process. Students alternate between listening and reporting.

- The focus might change for each rotation. For example: *Share your feelings about this topic … This time, share one fact you think is true about the topic … Now share one question you have about the topic …*

TEACHING POINTS

- This is a very useful context for assessment of speaking and listening skills as well as the unit content. Keep time limits short to ensure that the activity is well paced.

Conversation counters

This strategy is a useful way to assist students in learning how to take turns and to wait for others. It also encourages everyone to participate.

BASIC PROCEDURE

- Give each student in the group a set of 3 or 4 conversation counters (eg blocks or beads) and place a bowl in the middle of the discussion circle. Each time a student wishes to talk they must give up one of their conversation counters.

- Students attempt to use up all their counters during the course of the discussion.

- Once counters have been used, students may not make any further contributions

MODIFICATIONS

- Counters can also be color-coded for older students and linked to the kinds of contributions students make. For example:
    red = 1 question
    blue = 1 answer to a question
    yellow = a comment/response to someone else's idea

- These can also be used in small group work.

TEACHING POINTS

- This activity might not be successful first time – it takes practice! Allow students time to get used to using the counters in the discussion.

Cumulative listing

As individuals, pairs or small groups report back after a brainstorm, the recording process can become tedious. This strategy allows the reporting process to be worked through efficiently.

BASIC PROCEDURE

- After the activity has been completed, ask one student or group to share one of their ideas.

- Record ideas, then ask for others who had a similar response to raise their hands.

- Record the number of similar responses.

- Move to a new person or group and repeat the process until all ideas have been recorded.

- Not only does this streamline the sharing process, it provides interesting data about the frequency of ideas generated amongst the class.

MODIFICATIONS

- The same principle can be applied by asking students to display their work and then read across each groups' charts to glean the most common responses.

TEACHING POINTS

- This is a good exercise for encouraging active listening. Students only report back ideas that have not already been documented.

Discussion dissection

This strategy enables students to reflect on the dynamics of a whole-group discussion.

BASIC PROCEDURE

- Prior to a discussion session, consider an aspect that you or the students would like to be observed more closely. Points for observation could include:
  - the balance between contributions of girls and boys
  - the number of questions asked by the teacher compared to the number asked by students
  - the number of times someone interrupts someone else
  - those who make contributions during a discussion and those who do not
  - the responses given by the teacher and students to points made during a discussion
- Nominate a small group of students to make notes or keep a tally during discussion over a day.
- Ask students to then share results with the class and discuss.
- Consider ways to improve discussions based on the data gathered.
- Redo the observations at a later stage and compare results

MODIFICATIONS

- Record the discussion on video or audio tape and analyse it with students afterwards.

TEACHING POINTS

- You may choose to do your initial observations without telling the students, but it is generally more effective to make the data collection explicit.

Focused reporting

The sharing of group work can become tedious if each group report is too long or detailed. Try using these techniques for focusing the reports.

BASIC PROCEDURE

- Ask students to choose two important points from their discussion to share with the rest of the class.

- They then prioritise the list they have come up with and report back the first and last item on the list.

- They have two minutes to share their ideas with the class. As a group, they rehearse what they will say given the time available.

- Students then summarise their ideas in one statement or a diagram and display it for others to see.

Jigsaw sharing

The grouping strategy used for expert groups (see page 93) can be applied to any group situation for sharing purposes. Individual members from each home group meet to form new sharing groups. They report back on their home group's work.

Talking stick

The talking stick works on a similar principle to the conversation counters and is particularly effective with younger students.

BASIC PROCEDURE

- An object (such as a decorated stick or wand) is passed to the student who wishes to speak.

- Only those with the talking stick can speak.

- A rule can be established that only allows the stick to be passed to each person once.

Print walk

This is similar to 'carousel sharing' but with a less structured approach. It can be used regularly during the unit to encourage students to recap and reflect on the work done so far.

BASIC PROCEDURE

- Work produced by groups or individuals (as a result of one or more activities) is displayed around the room.

- The class is instructed to walk around the room, reading and viewing the work.

- They may be given a focus question to guide their observations, for example: *What patterns do you notice as you read through people's ideas?* or *Find one thing that surprises you.*

- Print walk can be conducted regularly during the unit to revise where you have been so far.

MODIFICATIONS

- Try a silent print walk – reporting back on patterns and points of interest after the walk.

TEACHING POINTS

- You might find it easiest to schedule small groups of students to carry out their print walk at specific times during a session or day.

- Combine a print walk with the use of feedback cards. Each student is given a card with one other student's (or group's) name on it. They are required to write down three responses to the work of that student or group.

Watch this space

This is a fun way of conducting a whole-class discussion and also allows students to observe a discussion in progress. Teachers play an important managerial role in implementing this strategy.

BASIC PROCEDURE

- Set up two circles of chairs or cushions – a small inner circle and an outer circle.

- A small group self-selects or is selected to begin in the inner circle. They are given a particular topic to discuss.

- Other students sit in the outer circle and observe the discussion for a set period of time but may not interrupt.

- Students in the outer circle who wish to have a say must raise their hand.

- When given the signal by the teacher, selected individuals from the outer circle may tap someone on the shoulder in the inner circle who must vacate their chair.

- Once the space is vacated, they join the inner circle to enter the discussion.

- Students who have been largely observing the discussion report back on what they noticed about issues raised and discussion strategies used.

MODIFICATIONS

- A 'fishbowl' discussion can also be used where the two circles remain fixed and students in the outer circle are given specific observation points, for example: *Observe the body language people use when they are trying to persuade someone else.*

STRATEGIES FOR REFLECTION AND SELF-ASSESSMENT

The following strategies can be carried out throughout the unit of work. In addition to these, many of the strategies outlined in chapter 4 can be used on a regular basis.

Class diary

This is similar to a learning log, but it is a record kept by the whole class.

BASIC PROCEDURE

- Using a scrap book or large book you have compiled for the purpose, keep a descriptive and reflective record of the key activities carried out during the unit.

- This can be done at the end of each day and written by the teacher (scribing students' ideas) or by individuals or small groups of students.

- Use two columns in the diary. In one column write a summary of what has been done. In the other, some comments about why it was done.

- The class journal can be illustrated by different students each day. Photographs and work samples may also be added to it.

Group work pie chart

BASIC PROCEDURE

- After groups have finished working on a shared task, provide each of them with a circle drawn on a large sheet of paper – or a copy of *Blackline master 4.*

- The group then fills out the circle in pie chart style to represent the relative contributions of each of the group members.

- Share pie charts and discuss their implications. For example, if there is a significant imbalance between the contributions of certain members, how could this be better managed next time?

MODIFICATIONS

- Students could choose other forms of visual representation to demonstrate their reflections on the group work process (using symbols, scoring systems, graphs etc).

TEACHING POINTS

- It is important for students to learn to discuss the effective ways. The debriefing process after this activity is vital to its success and ensures that the reflections made are valid and thoughtful.

Learning logs

Learning logs, or thinking books, provide opportunities for students to regularly reflect on what and how they are learning and feeling as the unit unfolds. There are many ways to construct and use learning logs. They can be designed specifically for the unit on which you are working, or they can be a general log that is used across the curriculum and throughout the year. The logs can be very loosely structured – simply allowing time to write – or they can be more directed with, for example, a different focus question for each entry. The following procedure is one way of introducing learning logs. (From Hamston & Murdoch 1996.)

BASIC PROCEDURE

- Begin by modelling reflective writing through a whole-class learning log. At the end of key activities in a unit, gather the class together and jointly construct an entry. Alternatively, you could begin by modelling your own entries in a learning log – 'thinking aloud' as you write.

- Provide students with a set of focus questions for their own writing after a particular activity, for example:
  Write about something new that you learned today.
  How did you feel about this activity?
  Write about how well you worked today. What did you do well? What would you do differently if you were to do this again?
  What questions do you have about (the topic) at the moment?

- Provide written feedback to students about their entry. The learning logs can become an ongoing dialogue between teacher and student.

MODIFICATIONS

- Other structures can be used to assist students in writing their learning logs. Concept maps, diagrams, pictures, and so on can be used as alternative ways of sorting out or expressing their ideas.

Year 2 students share their learning logs in small groups.

TEACHING POINTS

- Encourage students to share their learning logs with others. Peers could also provide oral or written feedback.

- As students become more comfortable and confident with writing in their learning logs, you may provide less guidance by way of focus questions and encourage students, instead, to respond by expressing their thoughts in the way they feel is most appropriate.

Photojournals

Use photographs to help students reflect on both what and how they have learned throughout a unit.

BASIC PROCEDURE

- Take photographs of activities throughout the unit of work, including students working on tasks, work samples and other items produced during the unit, and key resources.

- At the end of the unit, ask students to help you organise the photographs in sequence.

- Now ask students to write, in pairs or small groups, a caption for each of the photographs. The captions must explain:
  - what the photograph is showing
  - the purpose of the activity
  - the way students felt about the activity

- A photograph album or photographic display can then be shared with parents and other members of the school community.

MODIFICATIONS

- Individual students could compile their own photographic record of the unit – although this can be an expensive exercise!

TEACHING POINTS

- Younger students may need you to scribe their ideas. Captions can be written as a whole class.

Reflection roundabouts

The use of a spiral shape in which to write reinforces the cyclical way we build learning over time. (Based on an idea in Davies, Politano & Cameron 1993.)

BASIC PROCEDURE

- Revise the unit activities using the procedures suggested for learning maps (see page 113).

- Provide students with *Blackline master 5.*

- Individually, students write around their spirals to represent their learning during the unit of work.

- Display and share the spirals.

- Ask students to consider why their responses may be different from those of others.

MODIFICATIONS

- The class could create a giant spiral as a whole-class reflection activity.

- Photographs and drawings can be added to the spiral.

- Larger spirals can be cut out and hung as a mobile.

- Once students have completed the spiral provided, they can create their own sentence beginnings for themselves and others to complete.

TEACHING POINTS

- Learning logs are a useful reference for students as they complete their spirals.

Self-assessment

An essential part of helping students learn – about the topic and about themselves as learners.

BASIC PROCEDURE

- There are many ways in which students can self-assess their progress in a unit of work. Some of the strategies already outlined in this book can be used for self-assessment purposes. These include learning logs and learning maps.

- By setting goals at the beginning and during the course of the unit, students will be better able to assess their progress.

- The tuning-in phase of a unit can include goal-setting activities, where students may suggest a list of skills and understandings they hope to have achieved by the end of the unit. This can be assisted by their teacher being explicit about the teaching and learning purposes within a unit.

- If students know what they have been working towards in a unit or even in one activity, they are in a better position to assess their progress.

- *Blackline masters 6* and *7* are included to assist students to self-assess their work throughout the unit.

MODIFICATIONS

- The sentence beginnings provided can be used in conjunction with other strategies such as:

  Finish the sentence (page 19)
  Question of the day (page 29)
  The question game (page 33)
  Topic wheels (page 36)
  Bloom's box (page 98)

This student spends some quiet time reflecting on her learning.

TEACHING POINTS

- Self-assessment is a skill that should be modelled to students and regularly practised by them. Use the structures suggested in this chapter as the basis for modelling your own self-assessment to students. Display the blackline masters on an overhead projector and show students how you would fill them in about yourself. Think aloud as you do so to encourage students to mimic the questions you ask yourself.

- Students should share their self-assessment ideas with each other, This encourages them to see that *everyone* has aspects of their work they wish to improve.

8

PUTTING IT ALL TOGETHER

This section provides two sample integrated units of work. 'Night and Day' is planned for young students in years 1 and 2. 'Water, Water Everywhere' is planned for students in the older grades. These units are designed to provide models of the way the strategies in this book can be linked together to form a sequence of inquiry-based activities that develop significant understandings and draw on a range of curriculum areas. Importantly, these sample units show some flexibility in the use of strategies from particular areas of the inquiry model. For example, mime – a sorting-out activity – has been used to tune in to the night and day topic.

The strategies are cross-referenced to their description in this book. Teachers devising their own unit plan may need to provide more detail in the planner itself. The proforma used for this plan has been adapted from Murdoch and Hornsby (1997) *Planning Curriculum Connections*. This reference also provides other ways of documenting integrated units of work. You are encouraged to develop your own proforma that suits your particular teaching context.

Sample unit 1

INTEGRATED UNIT PLANNER

Title: *Night and Day*   **Focus:**   *Cause of night and day, observation, shadows, life style*

Year level: *1 & 2*
Duration: *4 weeks*
Host content area: *Science and Study of society and environment*
Strands: *Earth and beyond; natural and social systems*
Teaching staff: *Astrida, Carol, Linda, Janice, Kath*

SKILLS

Analysing
Checking ✔
Classifying
Cooperating ✔
Considering options
Designing
Elaborating ✔
Estimating
Explaining ✔
Generalising
Hypothesising ✔
Inferring
Interpreting
Justifying
Listening
Locating information
Making choices
Note-taking
Observing ✔
Ordering events ✔
Organising
Performing
Persuading
Planning
Predicting
Presenting in a range of ways ✔
Providing feedback
Questioning
Reading
Recognising bias
Reflecting ✔
Reporting ✔
Responding to others' work
Restating
Revising ✔
Seeing patterns
Selecting information
Self-assessing ✔
Sharing ideas ✔
Summarising ✔
Synthesising
Testing
Viewing
Visually representing ✔
Working independently
Working to a timeline

Understandings

The way we live is influenced by the different characteristics of day and night.

The Sun gives us light, warmth and energy, and makes things grow.

The length of a shadow is determined by the position of the light source.

Shadows are formed when light is blocked.

Day and night are caused by the rotation and position of the Earth in relation to the Sun.

Related values/attitudes/issues

During this unit of work, we will be focusing on the children's confidence to inquire, investigate, explain, demonstrate and share. We wish to emphasise appropriate behavior when working in small groups. In expressing their conceptions of how night, day, shadow and light 'work' we will encourage children to take risks and self-assess as their understandings grow.

Key concepts (big ideas)

Cause and effect, energy, relationships

Sample unit 1 (continued)

Assessment routines and records: What needs to be set up at the beginning of the unit to ensure: • systematic collection of assessment data? • ongoing reflection and self-assessment? (see assessment plan)	*Set up individual <u>learning logs</u> for regular reflection throughout the unit.* *Regular <u>print walks</u> with individuals and small groups.* *Folios for diagrams, <u>effects wheels</u>, <u>2 trues and a false</u>, etc.* *Checklist for skills and anecdotal notes.*	*p. 145* *p. 142* *pp. 108, 119*

		Grouping:	
Tuning in and preparing to find out: What *variety* of activities will be used to: • engage all students in the topic? • assess prior knowledge? • refine further planning? • lead into the 'finding out' experiences?	<u>*Visual representation*</u>*: What 'causes' day and night? Children draw and label diagrams.*	*individual*	*p. 39*
	<u>*Finish the sentence*</u>*: In small groups children draw and write their responses to 'If there were no Sun …'*	*small groups*	*p. 19*
	<u>*Brainstorming*</u>*: Carry this out on a regular basis to generate a list of questions about night and day.*	*whole class*	*p. 12*
	<u>*Show what you know*</u>*: Children mime activities that can be done during the day and at night.*	*small groups*	*p. 63*
	<u>*Pass the ball*</u>*: Ideas about what the Sun does for us.*	*whole class*	*p. 24*

Classroom Connections © K. Murdoch 1998 (Eleanor Curtain Publishing)

Sample unit 1 (continued)

Finding out: Experiences to assist students to gather new information about the topic.	Sorting out: Activities to assist students to process and work with the information and ideas they have gathered about the topic (including exploring values).	
<u>Structured observations</u>: Children observe and record pictures and/or notes about day and night x 4 sessions each week of unit.	Daily <u>oral presentations</u> to share observations made at home. (language)	pp. 63, 84
	<u>Soundscape</u> using musical instruments to represent dawn, dusk, night, etc. (music)	p. 80
<u>Experiments</u>: Children measure changes in their shadow throughout a day.	<u>Graphs</u> using streamers to show changes in shadows at different times during the day. (maths)	pp. 52, 76
	<u>Shadow puppets</u> using overhead projector – create puppets of different sizes. (art)	p. 69
<u>Night box</u>: Children <u>experiment</u> with a torch and ball in a darkened room to work out cause of night and day.	Whole-class written <u>explanation</u> of why day becomes night. Create a <u>collage</u> to accompany the explanation. (language, art)	pp. 52, 81 p. 71
<u>Video</u> from STEPS program about night and day.	<u>Told us, made us wonder</u> chart to retrieve and record information from the video. (language)	pp. 53, 84
<u>Shared book experience</u>: Big book "One Day, One Night" (Steve Moline)	<u>Read and retell</u> sections from the book (in small groups) using <u>jigsaw</u> strategy. (language)	pp. 61, 86 p. 142

Making conclusions: Activities to 'pull it all together', to assist students to *demonstrate* what they have learned and *reflect* on their learning.		
	<u>Effects wheel</u>: 'Without the Sun ...' – students make their own effects wheels.	p. 108
	Revisit <u>diagrams</u>: Make changes or draw new diagrams to show what has been learned.	p. 73
	<u>Two trues and a false</u>: To test students' understanding of causes of day and night.	
	<u>Learning map</u>: using photographs, represent the learning journey experienced by the class in finding out about day and night.	p. 119

Process areas used (highlight):
Arts: dance, drama, media, music, visual arts
Maths: space, number, measurement, chance and data, tools and procedures
English: texts, contextual understanding, linguistic features and structures, strategies
Technology: materials, information, systems

Sample unit 1 (continued)

Going further: Activities to challenge and extend. (These may be in the form of further shared experiences, individual or group projects, etc.)	*Making simple sundials as a <u>cooperative group task</u>. Follow a set of instructions, experiment and write or draw conclusions.* *Individual <u>contracts</u> based on areas of interest as they arise during the unit (eg making models of Earth, Sun, Moon).*	*p. 92* *p. 91*
Action: Activities to link theory to practice. To empower children to act on what they have learned and make links to their daily lives.	*<u>Annotated exhibition</u> of children's work. Prepare <u>pamphlets</u> explaining the work to parents. Children act as tour guides to explain exhibition to guests.*	*p. 125* *p. 81*

Classroom Connections © K. Murdoch 1998 (Eleanor Curtain Publishing)

Sample unit 2

INTEGRATED UNIT PLANNER

Title: Water, water everywhere   **Focus:** Water Conservation

Year level: 4–6

Duration: 6 weeks

Host content area: Studies of society and the environment; science; health

Strands: Strands: Place and space; resources; natural and social systems (also life and living and health of human populations)

Teaching staff: Kath and Fiona

SKILLS
Analysing ✔
Checking
Classifying
Cooperating ✔
Considering options ✔
Designing
Elaborating
Estimating
Explaining
Generalising
Hypothesising
Inferring
Interpreting
Justifying
Listening
Locating information ✔
Making choices
Note-taking
Observing
Ordering events
Organising ✔
Performing
Persuading ✔
Planning
Predicting
Presenting in a range of ways ✔
Providing feedback
Questioning ✔
Reading
Recognising bias
Reflecting
Reporting
Responding to others' work
Restating
Revising
Seeing patterns ✔
Selecting information ✔
Self-assessing ✔
Sharing ideas
Summarising
Synthesising
Testing
Viewing ✔
Visually representing ✔
Working independently ✔
Working to a timeline ✔

Understandings

Living things, including humans depend on water for their survival.

Water provides an important habitat and food source for many living things.

As it moves through its cycle, water is changed by both human and natural processes.

There are systems that have been set up to carry waste and excess water; pollutants that end up in these systems are carried out to sea.

Because it is essential to life, water needs to be conserved and protected.

There are ways we can modify our lifestyle to protect and conserve water.

There are many communities in the world where access to fresh water is limited by economic and social inequity.

Related values/attitudes/issues

This unit of work is designed to help students develop an appreciation of our dependence on water for survival. Through exploring the role water plays in sustaining life on earth, and examining our daily use of water we hope to engender in students a sense of personal responsibility for maintaining the health of this important natural resource. Using water wisely is something in which children can personally engage and act. We are hoping that the students will see ways in which their own water use can be modified — starting at the school level. The unit also expands to a global perspective and explores the inequity between people in different parts of the world in relation to their access to fresh water. The unit is designed to explore the relationship between social justice in relation to world health.

Key concepts (big ideas)
Cycles, systems, dependence, sustainability, pollution, conservation, equity

Sample unit 2 (continued)

Resources: What material do we need to help us plan and teach this topic?	Video and curriculum kit: *Drains to the Bay*, Melbourne Water K. Murdoch & S. Ray, *Waterways*, Macmillan, 1995 Websites in water education, eg: http://www.schnet.edu.au/Yarra Water/csfmain.htm R. Heimann, *A City by the River*, OUP, Melbourne 1987 Community Aid Abroad information on water distribution around the world *Waterworks!* by Beth Gilligan and Clare Bleakley, Australian Catholic Relief, Sydney The Water Story Information Sheets available from Australian Conservation Foundation Video material from World Vision
Assessment routines and records: What needs to be set up at the beginning of the unit to ensure: • systematic collection of assessment data? • ongoing reflection and self-assessment? (see assessment plan)	Skills checklist to document individual progress throughout the unit of work. A3 grid to make anecdotal notes about children (one grid per each week for the unit) Whole class reflective learning log to be kept throughout the unit. Video camera to record activities throughout the unit. Self-assessment activities at regular times throughout the unit. Portfolios for key work samples.

		Grouping:	
Tuning in and preparing to find out: What variety of activities will be used to: • engage all students in the topic? • assess prior knowledge? • refine further planning? • lead into the 'finding out' experiences?	<u>Cover puzzle</u> using large photo of wetland environment. Once the picture is revealed, ask children, What can you tell me about this place? Use <u>talking stick strategy</u> to share ideas about wetlands	whole class	p. 18 p. 142
	<u>Visual representation</u> of what happens to a piece of litter dropped onto the school ground and swept down a drain.	pairs	p. 39
	Use plasticine to make <u>models</u> of plants and animals that live in and around wetland areas.	small groups	p. 72
	How does the water get to the tap? Where does it go when it goes down the sink? Show using <u>mime and movement</u>.	small groups	p. 68
	<u>Bundling</u> activity: brainstorm and group words about water pollution.	small groups	p. 14
	List <u>questions</u> for guest speaker.	whole class	p. 47
	<u>Possible sentences</u> activity using text from *Waterways*	individual	p. 27
	On a <u>map</u> of Australia, <u>draw</u> where you think the main water bodies are	individual	p. 77

Sample unit 2 (continued)

Finding out: Experiences to assist students to gather new information about the topic.	Sorting out: Activities to assist students to process and work with the information and ideas they have gathered about the topic (including exploring values).	
<u>Video</u>: *Drains to the Bay* showing the way litter, oil etc dropped in the streets ends up in the bay.	Revisit <u>diagrams and models</u> made at the tuning-in stage. What should we modify? How have our ideas changed? (art)	pp. 53, 73, 72
<u>Guest speaker</u> from local water authority to talk about how water is stored and transported to and from our homes.	<u>Whole class report</u> (shared text construction activity) based on the information gathered from the guest speaker. Return to questions and consider what we have learned. (English)	p. 47
<u>Shared book experience</u>: big book *Waterways*.	<u>Cloze</u> activity focusing on the content-based words in the text. Revisit <u>possible sentences</u> and ways they can now be modified. (English)	pp. 61, 103 p. 27
<u>Survey</u> of families water use at home and school. Students design and carry out the surveys over 2 weeks.	<u>Role-play</u> activity — debate over a factory that is polluting local waterways with waste product from its manufacturing process. Roles include local resident, fisher, factory owner, factory employee, department of conservation representative. (drama)	pp. 54, 69 p. 50
<u>Excursion</u> to local wetland area. Read *A City by the River*.	Tally results from survey and enter on spreadsheets. Use computer programs to create <u>visual summaries and representation</u> of data. What does it tell us? Conduct a <u>fact finding</u> activity to compare the national average water use with our won. Calculate water used by each activity over a day, week, month, year. How can we save water? (maths)	p. 39 p. 75
Letters to local water authorities; Community Aid Abroad and other relevant organisations.	Make a <u>musical story</u> to accompany the scenes and timeline shown in *A City by the River*. (music)	p. 80
	Create <u>dioramas</u> to show aspects of wetland as habitat to certain plants and animals. (art)	p. 71

Making conclusions: Activities to 'pull it all together', to assist students to *demonstrate* what they have learned and *reflect* on their learning.	Use <u>Bloom s box</u> activity to test children s developing knowledge and understanding about the topic.	p. 98
	<u>Concept map</u> showing the links between key concepts related to use and conservation of water.	p. 99
	<u>Cross impact grid</u> to demonstrate understanding of the way certain activities impact on waterways.	p. 104
	<u>Similes and metaphors</u>: Waterways are like ; The storm water system is like ; Water is to the earth what is to our bodies. Children create their own.	p. 114
	<u>What am I</u> — focusing on animals that live in water.	p. 121

Process areas used (highlight):
Arts: dance, drama, media, music, visual arts
Maths: space, number, measurement, chance and data, tools and procedures
English: texts, contextual understanding, linguistic features and structures, strategies
Technology: materials, information, systems

Sample unit 2 (continued)

Going further: Activities to challenge and extend. (These may be in the form of further shared experiences, individual or group projects, etc.)	Small group <u>contract work</u> to focus on water availability, use and distribution in various communities around the world (location, availability, sanitation etc).	p. 91
	<u>Internet search</u> to examine sites about water conservation around the world. If possible link up with GREEN network on Interknit to find out about international water pollution prevention (http://www.igc.apc.org/green/green.html)	p. 64
	<u>7 at once</u> creative thinking activity focusing on possible solutions to preserving waterways around the world.	p. 94
Action: Activities to link theory to practice. To empower children to act on what they have learned and make links to their daily lives.	Possible class involvement in GREEN project.	
	Design posters or pamphlets to promote conservation of water.	
	<u>Personal pledges</u> to care for waterways and reduce consumption.	p. 132
	Presentation to school council — <u>action plan</u> for water management in the school community.	p. 128

A MENU FOR PLANNING AND RECORD-KEEPING

About the menu...

This menu lists all the strategies outlined in the book. It will provide you with an overview of strategies for quick reference during planning and evaluation. The menu includes columns in which you can record strategies used in various units throughout the year. This will help you to reflect on the balance across types of strategies you introduce to students and on the opportunities students have had for repetition and practice.

In each section, space has been left for you to add your own strategies. Following the menu is a photocopiable proforma to record the procedures, modifications and teaching points for new strategies. Make these available to the whole staff and use them to share ideas.

TUNING IN	Page	Unit	Unit	Unit	Unit	Unit	Unit	Unit	Unit
• Brainstorming	12								
• Bundling	14								
• Chatterboxes	16								
• Cover puzzles	18								
• Finish the sentence	19								
• Graffiti board	19								
• Mind mapping	20								
• Mystery boxes	22								
• Paired interviews	23								
• Pass the ball	24								
• People bingo	25								
• Picture priorities	26								
• Possible sentences	27								
• Post-a-question	28								
• Question of the day	29								
• Rocket writing	29								
• Silent jigsaw	30								
• Something from home	31								
• Startling statements	32								
• The question game	33								
• Think, pair, share	34								
• Think, wink, decide	35								
• Topic wheels	36								
• Visualisation and prediction	37								
• Visual representation *labelled diagrams comic strips plasticine models collages 3D models maps/floor plans flow diagrams cut-away/X-ray pictures*	39								
• Word association and definitions	41								
•									
•									
•									

FINDING OUT	Page	Unit	Unit	Unit	Unit	Unit	Unit	Unit	Unit
• Animals and plants in the classroom	45								
• Ask an expert	47								
• CD ROM	48								
• Excursions	50								
• Experiments	52								
• Film, video and television	53								
• Interviews and surveys	54								
• Letter writing	56								
• Newspapers and magazines	57								
• Paintings, photographs, drawings and other visual images	58								
• Picture books and novels	59								
• Phone calls	61								
• Shared book experience	61								
• Structured observations	63								
• The Internet	64								
•									
•									
•									
•									
•									
•									
•									
•									
•									
•									
•									
•									
•									
•									
•									
•									

SORTING OUT	Page	Unit	Unit	Unit	Unit	Unit	Unit	Unit	Unit
(a) Through dance and drama...									
• Conscience game	68								
• Free movement	68								
• Freeze frame	68								
• Mime	68								
• Puppet plays	69								
• Role-play	69								
• Simulations	71								
• Talk shows	70								
•									
•									
•									
•									
•									
•									
(b) Through media and visual arts									
• Collage	71								
• Dioramas	71								
• Models	72								
• Visual artwork *paint, crayon, charcoal, pencils, pastels, chalk*	72								
• Diagrams *X-ray, comic strips, flow charts, cut-aways, maps, before-and-after*	73								
• Using fabrics *quilts, patchwork, wall hangings, puppets, table cloths, dolls and other figures*	73								
• Making videos	73								
• Multimedia presentations	74								
• Mobiles	74								
• Radio plays	74								
• Thaumatropes	75								
•									
•									

SORTING OUT	Page	Unit	Unit	Unit	Unit	Unit	Unit	Unit	Unit
(c) Through mathematics									
• Classifying	75								
• Fact finding	75								
• Graphs	76								
pictographs, pie graphs, line graphs, bar graphs, 3D graphs, dot graphs, stem plots									
• Maps	77								
• Maths projects	76								
• Problem-solving	77								
• Scale models and drawings	78								
• Timelines	78								
• Venn diagrams	78								
•									
•									
•									
•									
•									
•									
•									
•									
(d) Through music									
• Chants	79								
• Composition	80								
• Musical stories	80								
• Raps	79								
• Round the camp fire	79								
• Soundscapes	80								
•									
•									
•									
•									
•									
•									

SORTING OUT	Page	Unit	Unit	Unit	Unit	Unit	Unit	Unit	Unit
(e) Through English									
• Bookmaking	87								
• Build a story	82								
• Compare and contrast	82								
• Data charts	82								
• DRTA	83								
• Oral presentations	84								
• Poetry	86								
• Readers theatre	87								
• Read and retell	86								
• Puzzle cards	87								
• Three-level guides	86								
• Told us... made us wonder	84								
• Wall stories/charts	85								
• Writing using a range of text types	81								
Personal descriptions									
Technical descriptions									
Scientific reports									
Explanations									
Instructions									
Manuals									
Recipes									
Directions									
Reviews									
Diaries									
Personal recounts									
Stories									
Fables									
Fairy tales									
Poems									
Letters									
Advertisement									
Charts									
Scripts									
Banners									
• Written conversation	85								
•									
•									
•									
SORTING OUT USING TECHNOLOGY									
investigating, designing, producing, evaluating	88								
•									
•									
•									
•									

Classroom Connections © K. Murdoch 1998 (Eleanor Curtain Publishing)

GOING FURTHER	Page	Unit	Unit	Unit	Unit	Unit	Unit	Unit	Unit
• Contracts	91								
• Cooperative groups task	92								
• Expert groups	93								
• Individual projects	90								
• Seven-at-once	94								
•									
•									
•									
•									
•									
•									
•									
•									
•									
•									
•									
•									
•									
•									
•									

MAKING CONCLUSIONS	Page	Unit	Unit	Unit	Unit	Unit	Unit	Unit	Unit
• Board games	97								
• Bloom's box	98								
• Concept maps	99								
• Connectit	101								
• Consensus 1-3-6	104								
• Content-based cloze	103								
• Cross impact grid	104								
• Crossword puzzles	105								
• De Bono's 6 thinking hats	107								
• Diamond display	106								
• Effects wheels	108								
• In my club	110								
• Laying it in the line	111								
• Learning maps	113								
• PMI	115								
• Putting you in the picture	116								
• Question ball	117								
• Question me an answer	118								
• Similies and metaphors	114								
• Statements of generalisation	118								
• Two trues and a false	119								
• Time capsules	120								
• What am I?	121								
•									
•									
•									
•									
•									
•									
•									
•									
•									
•									

TAKING ACTION	Page	Unit	Unit	Unit	Unit	Unit	Unit	Unit	Unit
• Advertising campaigns	124								
• Annotated exhibitions	125								
• Arts in the local community	126								
• Designing walks	126								
• Develop an action plan	128								
• From here to there	129								
• Global links	130								
• Hear all about it	131								
• Letter writing	131								
• Meet the press	132								
• Personal pledge	132								
• Read all about it	133								
• More strategies for action *Fund raising* *Publishing* *Signs* *Sponsoring* *Auditing* *Student representative council*	134								
•									
•									
•									
•									
•									
•									
•									
•									
•									
•									
•									
•									
•									
•									

STRATEGIES FOR PROMOTING REFLECTION AND DISCUSSION	Page	Unit	Unit	Unit	Unit	Unit	Unit	Unit	Unit	Unit
(A) Sharing and discussion										
• Carousel sharing	137									
• Class meetings	138									
• Concentric circles	138									
• Conversation counters	140									
• Cumulative listing	140									
• Discussion dissection	141									
• Focused reporting	142									
• Jigsaw sharing	142									
• Talking stick	142									
• Print walk	142									
• Watch that space	143									
•										
•										
•										
•										
•										
•										
•										
(B) Reflection and self-assessment										
• Class diary	144									
• Group work pie chart	144									
• Learning logs	145									
• Photojournals	146									
• Reflection roundabouts	146									
• Self-assessment	147									

PROFORMA FOR RECORDING NEW STRATEGIES

Name of strategy:	**Designed by:**

Brief description:

Most appropriate stage of unit:

Basic procedure:

Modifications:

Teaching points:

Name of strategy:	**Designed by:**

Brief description:

Most appropriate stage of unit:

Basic procedure:

Modifications:

Teaching points:

BLACKLINE MASTER 1
People Bingo

Find someone who ...	Find someone who ...	Find someone who ...
Find someone who ...	Find someone who ...	Find someone who ...
Find someone who ...	Find someone who ...	Find someone who ...
Find someone who ...	Find someone who ...	Find someone who ...

BLACKLINE MASTER 2
Topic Wheel

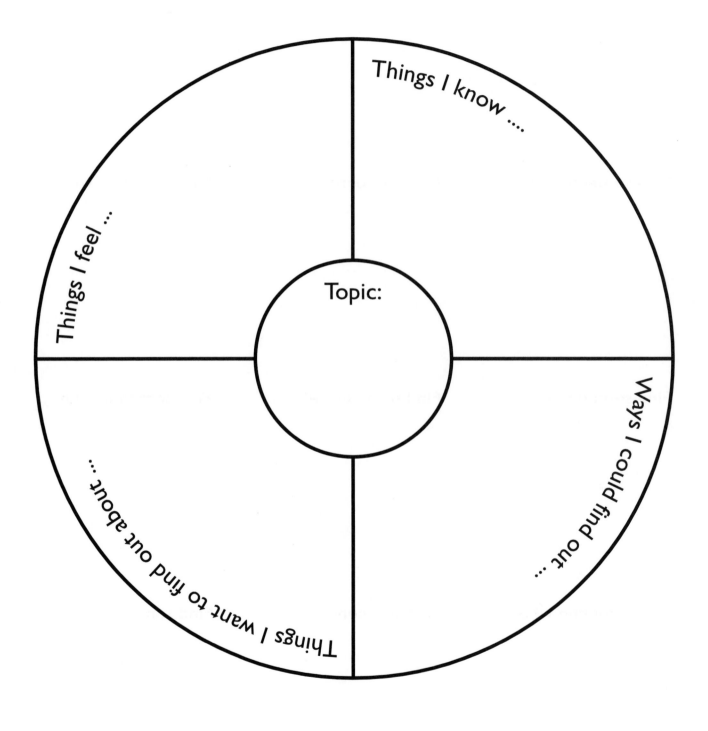

BLACKLINE MASTER 3
Preparing for our excursion

Name/s: _____

Draw something you think you will see.	**Make a list of sounds you expect to hear.**
Write about how you think you will feel.	**List two questions you would like answered.**

Now compare your ideas with a friends. In what ways are they the same and different? Why?

BLACKLINE MASTER 4
Reflecting on group work

Names: _____

1. How well did your group share the responsibilities for completing your task? As a group, fill in the pie chart to show the contributions of individuals in the group. You must all agree on the final chart.

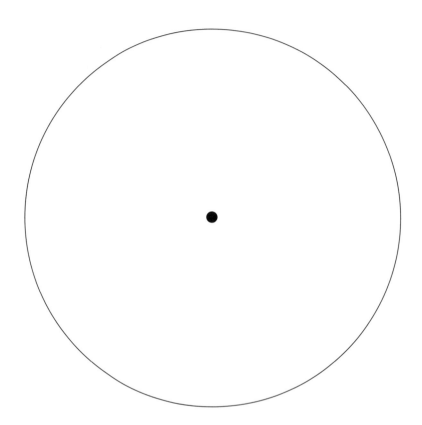

2. Now think about the way you worked as a group and give yourself a score out of ten for each of the following areas:

Taking turns   /10

Listening to each other   /10

Giving each other feedback   /10

Keeping to time   /10

Sharing the responsibility   /10

Solving problems   /10

Producing good work   /10

BLACKLINE MASTER 5
Reflection round-about

Think about what you have learned during our unit. Read around the spiral and finish the sentences.

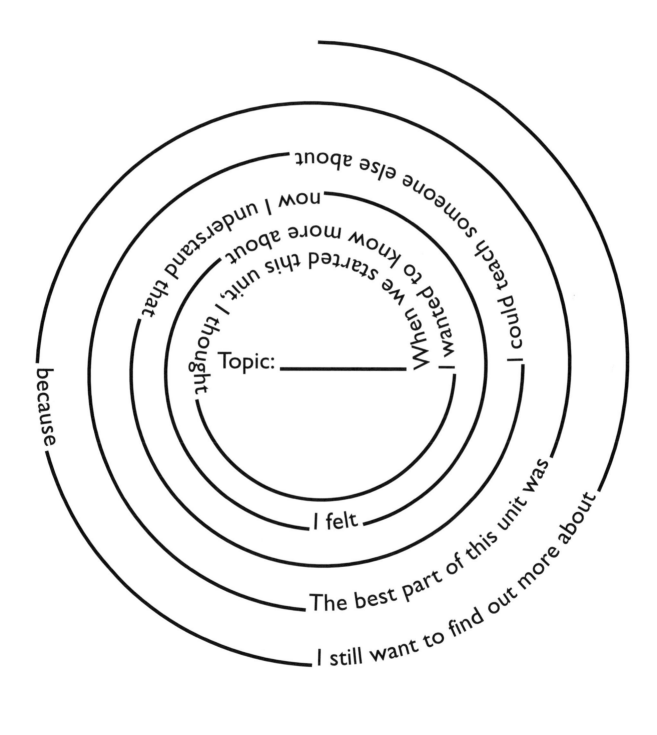

BLACKLINE MASTER 6
Reflecting on my learning 1

Unit topic: Name: _____

1. Three things I have learned about _____ are:

   •

   •

   •

2. The most important thing I have learned about _____ is

3. During the unit I felt _____ because

4. Something I have learned about myself as a learner is:

5. The best activity we did was _____ because

6. Something I need to improve is

7. I would like to find out more about

BLACKLINE MASTER 7
Reflecting on my learning 2

1. What did I like doing?	2. What didn't I like doing?
3. What did I do well?	4. What didn't I do so well?

1. Think about the work we have done in this unit of work.
   List the things you liked and didn't like in boxes 1 and 2.

2. Now think about the things from each list that you did well and not so well.
   Write those in boxes 3 and 4.

3. Share your grid with a friend and discuss:
   • What patterns do you notice? Are you only good at things you like?
   • What kinds of things do you do best?
   • What would you like to get better at doing?

Appendix 1

RESOURCES FOR THE INTEGRATED CLASSROOM

To be able to work effectively with many of the strategies suggested in this book, it is important to have resource materials on hand – for both student and teacher use. The lists below provide some guidance to the kinds of materials that are used in integrated classrooms. Naturally, many of these materials will need to be shared among classrooms but it is important to have them organised and available to teachers and students as the need arises. This saves a lot of time which that can otherwise be wasted asking or looking for things. Send a list of required materials home to parents and ask for donations.

GENERAL RESOURCES

address lists

assorted hats

atlas

calenders – including events coming up in the local community

camera

clipboards

collection of current and old magazines (for information and for art work)

computer

cushions (for small group discussions)

daily newspaper – bring your own or ask a parent to donate theirs the following day

envelopes, stamps

Internet guides

lists of local organisations

manilla folders or scrap books (for portfolios)

old calenders (for photos)

old phones (for dramatic activities)

phone books

photograph albums

plastic envelopes

post-it notes (very useful for lots of activities)

postcodes books

state map

street directories

tape recorders

world map

attribute blocks

TECHNOLOGY, MATHS, CONSTRUCTION MATERIALS

boxes of different shapes and sizes

calculators

commercially produced construction equipment (eg Lego)

compasses

computers

drinking straws

grid paper

icy-pole sticks

measuring jugs

rulers (metre and small)

Stanley knife

staple gun

stencils for basic shapes

sticky tape

tape measures

thermometers

trundle wheels

various containers

wooden off-cuts

ARTS/WRITING MATERIALS

Blu Tack

brushes and rollers

candles (for 'mood setting' during stories, etc)

cardboard

cellophane

charcoal

colored paper squares

colored pencils

crayons

drawing pins

dress-ups (for all age groups)

easel – for shared writing and big-book displays

large sheets of paper

lead pencils

masking tape

material scraps

non-permanent markers

old greeting cards

overhead projection sheets

paints

paper clips

paste

pastels

pens and pencils (assorted)

plasticine

raffia

rags

ready-cut cards for words and sentences

scissors

scrap paper

sponges

stamps and stamp pads

sticky labels

string

textas

tissue paper

wood glue

wool

APPENDIX 2
Skills often used at each stage of a unit

Stage of unit	Sample skills often required for effective use of these strategies
Tuning in	Decision-making • Estimating • Grouping • Hypothesising • Listening • Organising • Planning • Predicting • Prioritising • Questioning • Representing ideas visually • Sharing ideas with others
Finding out	Communicating • Comparing and contrasting • Extracting main ideas • Inferring • Listening • Locating and selecting relevant information • Note-taking • Observing • Organising • Questioning • Reading • Recognising bias • Scanning • Summarising • Viewing
Sorting out	Analysing • Classifying • Comparing and contrasting • Designing • Elaborating • Explaining • Expressing opinions, feelings and values • Interpreting information • Justifying • Making choices • Organising • Performing • Persuading • Presenting ideas to others • Reporting • Representing ideas in a range of ways • Responding to the work of others • Seeing patterns • Selecting appropriate materials • Testing and checking • Thinking creatively • Working cooperatively • Working with in a time limit

NAMES

Adapted from Murdoch & Hornsby 1997

APPENDIX 2 (continued)
Skills often used at each stage of a unit

Stage of unit	Going further	Making conclusions	Taking action
Sample skills often required for effective use of these strategies	Challenging Cooperating with others Comparing and contrasting Elaborating Evaluating Locating information Negotiating Revising Working independently Working to a time limit	Accepting and responding to feedback Elaborating Generalising Interpreting Linking cause and effect Modifying Ordering events Providing feedback Reflecting Restating Revising Self-assessing Summarising Synthesising Testing	Communicating with range of audiences Communicating appropriately for different purposes Considering options Justifying Performing Persuading Planning Presenting Prioritising Reflecting Working to a time line
NAMES			

Adapted from Murdoch & Hornsby 1997

REFERENCES AND FURTHER READING

Atkin, J. 1993, 'How students learn: a framework for effective teaching', IARTV seminar series no. 22, February, Melbourne.

Atkin, J. 1997, 'Stimulating and integrating your whole brain processing: going beyond preference to capacity', paper presented at Using Your Brain conference, World Congress Centre, Melbourne, January 22–4.

Ausubel, D. 1968, *Learning Theory and Classroom Practice*, Ontario Institute for Studies in Education, Toronto.

Baird, J. & Mitchell, I. (eds) 1986, *Improving the Quality of Teaching and Learning: An Australian Case Study – the PEEL project*, Monash University, Melbourne.

Baker, D., Semple, C. & Stead, T. 1990, *How Big is the Moon?* Oxford University Press, Melbourne.

Barmby, S. & Jones, K. 1991, *Assisting Learners: A Holistic Approach to Literacy Improvement*, Ringwood School Support Centre, Ringwood, Vic.

Beane, J. 1991, 'Problems and possibilities for an integrative curriculum', in *Integrating the Curricula: A Collection*, R. Fogarty (ed), Hawker Brownlow, Melbourne. pp 69–84.

Behar-Horenstein, L. 1994 'What's worth knowing for teachers?', *Educational Horizons*, Fall, 1994, pp 37–47.

Board of Studies 1995, *Curriculum and Standards Framework*, Board of Studies (Victoria), Melbourne.

Bruner, J. 1960, *The Process of Education*, Harvard University Press, Cambridge MA.

Caine, R. & Caine, G. 1990 'Understanding a brain-based approach to learning and teaching', *Educational Leadership*, vol 48, no 2, pp 66–70.

Cam, P. 1995, *Thinking Together: Philosophical Inquiry in the Classroom*, PETA and Hale & Iremonger, Sydney.

Cambourne, B. 1988, *The Whole Story: Natural Learning and the Acquisition of Literacy in the Classroom*, Ashton Scholastic, Gosford, NSW.

Cohen, D. 1987, 'The use of concept maps to represent unique thought processes: towards meaningful learning', *Journal of Curriculum and Supervision*, vol 2, no 3.

Cohen, D., Mclaughlin, M. & Talbert, J. (eds) 1993, *Teaching for Understanding: Challenges for Policy and Practice*, Jossey-Bass, San Francisco.

Collis, M. & Dalton, J. 1991, *Becoming Responsible Learners: Strategies for Positive Classroom Management*, Eleanor Curtain, Melbourne.

Dalton, J. & Smith, D. 1986, *Extending Children's Special Abilities: Strategies for Primary Classrooms*, Ministry of Education, Victoria.

Davies, A., Politano, C. & Cameron, C. 1993, *Making Themes Work*, Peguis, Winnipeg.

De Bono, E. 1976, *CoRT Thinking I–IV*, Pergamon Press, London.

De Bono, E. 1985, *Six Thinking Hats*, Penguin, Harmondsworth.

Derewianka, B. 1990, *Exploring How Texts Work*, PETA, Sydney.

Fatouros, C. & Walters-Moore, C. 1997, *Using Software in English*, PETA, Sydney.

Feden, P. 1994, 'About instruction: powerful new strategies worth knowing', *Educational Horizons*, Fall, pp 18–24.

Fogarty, R. (ed.) 1993, *Integrating the Curricula: A Collection*, Hawker Brownlow, Melbourne.

Fogarty, R., Perkins, D. & Barell, J. 1991, *How to Teach for Transfer*, Hawker Brownlow, Melbourne.

Gardner, H. 1983, *Frames of Mind: The Theory of Multiple Intelligences*, Basic Books, New York.

Gardner, H. 1997, Reflections on multiple intelligences: myths and messages, paper presented at Using Your Brain conference, World Congress Centre, Melbourne, January 22–24.

Goodlad, J. 1983, 'A study of schooling: some findings and hypotheses', *Phi Delta Kappa,* vol 64, March, p 467.

Goodman, K. 1986, *What's Whole in Whole Language?* Ashton Scholastic, Gosford, NSW.

Green, P. 1992, *A Matter of Fact: Using Factual Texts in the Classroom*, Eleanor Curtain, Melbourne.

Gunstone, R. & White, R. 1992, *Probing Understanding*, The Falmer Press, London.

Hamston, J. & Murdoch, K. 1996, *Integrating Socially: Units of Work for Social Education*, Eleanor Curtain, Melbourne.

Harste, J. 1992 'Inquiry-based instruction', *Primary Voices* K–6, vol 1, no 1, pp 2–5

Harste, J. Woodward, V. & Burke C. 1984, *Language Stories and Literacy Lessons*, Heinemann, Portsmouth NH.

Hayes-Jacobs, H. 1989, 'Design options for an integrated curriculum' in *Intedisciplinary Curriculum: Design and Implementation*, ed. H. Hayes-Jacobs, Association for Supervision and Curriculum Development, Alexandria, VA, pp 13–24.

Hill, S. 1991, *Readers Theatre: Performing the Text*, Eleanor Curtain, Melbourne.

Hornsby, D., Parry, J. & Sukarna, D. 1992, *Teach On*, Phoenix Education, Melbourne.

Lazear, D. 1994, *Multiple Intelligences Approaches to Assessment: Solving the Assessment Conundrum,* Hawker Brownlow, Melbourne.

Lipman, M. 1988, *Philosophy Goes to School*, Temple University Press, Philadelphia.

Ministry of Education 1985, *Destination Decisions: Decision-Making Strategies for School Communities*, Ministry of Education, Victoria.

Moline, S. 1995, *I See What You Mean*, Addison-Wesley Longman, Melbourne.

Murdoch, K. 1992, *Integrating Naturally: Units of Work for Environmental Education*, Dellasta, Melbourne.

Murdoch, K. 1993, *Springboards: Ideas for Environmental Education*, Nelson, Melbourne.

Murdoch, K. & Hornsby, D. 1997, *Planning Curriculum Connections*, Eleanor Curtain, Melbourne.

Novak, J. & Gowin, D. 1984, *Learning How to Learn*, Cambridge University Press, Cambridge.

Osborne, R. & Freyberg, P. 1985, *Learning in Science*, Heinemann, Auckland.

Perkins, D. 1993, 'The connected curriculum', *Educational Leadership*, October, pp 90–1.

Pigdon, K. & Woolley, M. (eds) 1992, *The Big Picture: Integrating Children's Learning*, Eleanor Curtain, Melbourne.

Pike, G. & Selby, D. 1988, *Global Teacher, Global Learner*, Hodder & Staughton, London.

Rosenshine, B. 1996, 'Synthesis of research on explicit teaching', *Educational Leadership*, April, pp 60–9.

Short, K. & Harste, J. (with C. Burke) 1996, *Creating Classrooms for Authors and Inquirers*, Heinemann, Portsmouth NH.

Short, K., Schroeder, J., Laird, J., Kauffman, G., Ferguson, M. & Crawford, K. 1996, *Learning Together through Inquiry: From Columbus to Integrated Curriculum*, Stenhouse, York, Maine.

Splitter, L. & Sharp, A. 1995, *Teaching for Better Thinking: The Classroom Community of Inquiry*, ACER, Melbourne.

State of Florida, Department of State 1996, *Florida Curriculum Framework*, Florida Department of Education, Tallahassee Florida.

Sukarna, D. Hornsby, D. & Jennings, C. 1996, *Planning for English: Outcomes in Context,* Eleanor Curtain, Melbourne.

White, R. & Gunstone, R. 1992, *Probing Understanding*, The Falmer Press, London.

Wilson, J. & Wing Jan, L.1993, *Thinking for Themselves*, Eleanor Curtain, Melbourne.

Wilson, L. 1991, *An Integrated Approach to Learning*, Nelson, Melbourne.

Wing Jan, L. 1991, *Write Ways: Modelling Writing Forms*, Oxford University Press, Melbourne.

INDEX OF STRATEGIES

PLANNING FOR ENGLISH
Outcomes in context
David Hornsby, Claire Jennings and Debbie Sukarna
ISBN 1 875327 37 1

PLANNING FOR THE KEY LEARNING AREAS
Outcomes in context
Claire Jennings and Julie Shepherd
ISBN 1 875327 43 6

PLANNING FOR MATHEMATICS
Outcomes in context
Rob Vingerhoets & Mick Ymer
ISBN 1 875327 44 4

The Planning Series provides a framework for planning in all key learning areas using outcome-based documents. It is appropriate for national and state curriculum documents and encompasses strands for levels 1 to 5.

The guided planning process in the series:

- helps you to build on existing quality teaching, learning and assessment practices and identify new ones
- links teaching and learning to authentic assessment contexts
- identifies important skills, strategies and behaviors in the integrated learning program
- demonstrates how assessment can be an integral part of planning
- presents a range of formats demonstrating quality program planning across the key learning areas.

The books provide guidance on commonly asked questions.

- How do I plan units of work?
- How do I cover all key learning areas?
- How do I monitor outcomes across the key learning areas?

- How do I plan according to content and process?
- Will I have time for individual student records?

The proformas which are an integral part of the planning books help you identify what you are already doing, relate it to current national and state curriculum documents and plan accordingly. The proformas also act as springboards for developing your own planning and record-keeping documents.

There are proformas for:

- planning a scope and sequence chart
- planning an integrated unit of work
- compiling individual student assessment records

PLANNING CURRICULUM CONNECTIONS
Planning with a purpose
KATH MURDOCH AND DAVID HORNSBY

Planning Curriculum Connections provides a planning model for developing an integrated curriculum.

Issues covered include:

- choosing worthwhile topics
- long-term planning – whole school and for all subject areas with sample scope and sequence charts provided
- planning effective integrated units of work
- planning for effective assessment and evaluation
- planning for teacher learning.

Proformas, sample scope and sequence charts and sample activities and timetables combine to provide useful, practical guidance.

ISBN 1 875327 49 5   *160 pp*

INTEGRATING SOCIALLY
Planning integrated units of work for social education
JULIE HAMSTON AND KATH MURDOCH

Integrating Socially is essentially a book about classroom practice. It provides a comprehensive and practical guide to developing integrated units of work for social education, incorporating a focus on language. It includes seven planned units on topics covering a broad spectrum of social education which serve as a resource for teaching and also act as models for teachers' own planning. The units have been designed to engage teachers and learners in shared investigations – developing critical understandings about the social world is seen as a shared enterprise between teacher and learner.

The contents:

- provide an overview of the theory that guides the practice
- outline the kind of content that should be covered in a comprehensive social education curriculum and provide information on how the units can be adapted to meet particular needs
- provide useful strategies for social education and describe different ways of learning which can be used in many different aspects of the school curriculum and applied to life beyond school
- include seven planned units which guide students through an explicit sequence of learning on topics dealing with significant and challenging issues
- explicit assistance in planning integrated units of work for social education.

ISBN 1 875327 36 3   *172 pp*

THE BIG PICTURE
Integrating children's learning
EDITED BY MARILYN WOOLLEY AND KEITH PIGDON

The Big Picture addresses the key issues which are central to the idea of the integrated curriculum and translates them into practical classroom advice.

Contents include:

- context and framework: the ideas which drive teachers' curriculum planning
- a planning model: bringing the components together in an organised yet flexible structure
- the model in practice: activities and strategies
- language and the integrated curriculum: integrated learning and specific curriculum practice
- assessment and evaluation: for the learner, the teacher and the community
- whole school change: it starts in your classroom.

ISBN 1 875327 14 2   *128 pp*

SPELLING
An Integrated Approach
WENDY BEAN AND CHRYS BOUFFLER

Many approaches to teaching spelling ignore the links between spelling, reading and writing. Wendy Bean and Chrys Bouffler outline a comprehensive method which takes into account the knowledge that spelling is the means of accessing reading and writing, which incorporates recent research and which provides strategies for success.

They believe that spelling is part of the process of language learning, that any aspect of language learning involves a complex interplay of forms and that spelling is not separate from reading and writing.

Spelling: An Integrated Approach provides:

- practical ideas for establishing the classroom environment
- strategies for establishing the guiding principles of a spelling program
- strategies to sensitise language learners to words in context
- a range of procedures to encourage writing and risk taking
- teaching procedures for proof reading together with proof reading activities
- a section on assessment and evaluation which includes guidelines for gathering data and for student self-evaluation.

ISBN 1 875327 45 2   *96 pp*

For further information about these or other titles contact:
Eleanor Curtain Publishing, 906 Malvern Road, Armadale, Vic 3143
Ph: 03-9822 0344   Fax: 03-9824 8851   Email: ecurtain@ozemail.com.au